Award-Winning Publicity

8 Media Boosters to Magnify your Story

Liz H. Kelly

AWARD-WINNING PUBLICITY
8 Media Boosters to Magnify Your Story
© Liz H Kelly 2026

Published by *Goody PR Press*
Goody PR (part of *Sunrise Road Media Inc.*)
Santa Monica, CA 90403
https://goodypr.com

ISBN Paperback: 979-8-234-02519-7
ISBN eBook: 979-8-234-02520-3

DEDICATION

This book is dedicated to my mother, Anne, who taught English at my high school for 30+ years —with passion —including teaching me and thousands of award-winning students who've won Oscars, actor and book awards.

This book is also dedicated to our friends, family, mentors, fellow publicists and clients who have supported our PR journey - every step of the way (see Acknowledgements).

And lastly, this book is dedicated to the *American Paper Optics (APO)* eclipse glasses team, John Jerit, CEO/Founder, Paulo Aur, CFO/COO/Co-Owner and Jason Lewin, CMO in Memphis, Tennessee, and their spokespeople, who worked tirelessly to make sure millions could safely watch and enjoy the April 8, 2024, Total Solar Eclipse.

SPECIAL THANKS

Sending special thanks *to* Beth Okeon (*ABO Marketing & Communications* Owner in Memphis), Wendy Guarisco (*Guarisco Group* CEO/Founder in Atlanta) and Jamie Feldstein (my first book publicist in Los Angeles), who through our connections led me to securing *APO* as a client for their national publicity campaign. Thank you Beth for referring me to *APO*, and thank you all for being great friends, mentors and cheerleaders on our PR journey!

GIVING BACK

A portion of our book profits from *Award-Winning Publicity* will be donated to autism charities and cancer research. F-Cancer!

PR is a Marathon,
Not a Sprint.

Be patient, persistent
and never desperate
in your publicity
journey.

– Liz H. Kelly,

*Goody PR and Goody Business Book Awards Founder
and Award-Winning Author*

This **Award-Winning Publicity** Book will feature Author **Liz H. Kelly's 6 PR Industry Awards** for **American Paper Optics / Eclipse Glasses National Publicity Campaign, including:**

- Best Publicity Campaign: 2025 *MarCom Awards*, Platinum Winner
- Best Public Relations Program: 2025 *MarCom Awards*, Platinum Winner
- Best Media Relations: 2024 *Bulldog PR Awards*, Top Gold Award Winner
- Platinum Grand Prix Award: 2024 *PRNews Platinum Awards*, Finalist
- Campaign – Other: 2024 *PRNews Platinum Awards*, Finalist
- Media Relations Campaign: 2024 *PR Daily Awards*, Finalist

TABLE OF **CONTENTS**

FOREWORD

Foreword by: **Jason Lewin**, Chief Marketing Officer (CMO)
American Paper Optics / EclipseGlasses.com

In the world of business, there are moments that define a company's legacy—moments where the window of opportunity is narrow, the stakes are astronomical, and there is absolutely zero room for error. At *American Paper Optics*, those moments were the historic North American Eclipses of 2023 and 2024.

As the world's leading manufacturer of safe solar eclipse glasses, our entire business cycle builds toward a few brief minutes of totality —when millions view a phenomenon in the sky where the Moon blocks the Sun. To the outside observer, it looks like a simple product launch. To us, it was a logistical and media marathon that required precision, relentless energy, and a voice that could cut through all the noise. We needed someone to pilot our rocket ship.

That is why we partnered with Liz Kelly of *Goody PR*.

I have been in this industry for a long time, and I know that a great product is only half the battle. The other half is storytelling, credibility, and the ability to command a room—or in our case, a national news cycle. From the moment Liz stepped into our orbit, it was clear she wasn't your average media relations manager. She was a strategist, a connector, and, most importantly, a great coach.

In this *Award-Winning Publicity* book, Liz talks about what it means to build your brand story, and I can tell you firsthand that she lives every chapter of this book. I watched her transform our team through intensive media coaching, turning technical experts into polished spokespeople ready for the spotlight. She didn't just "get us interviews"; she opened doors to industry leaders and key media stakeholders that allowed us to put over 75 million eclipse glasses into the hands of the public.

One of the things you will discover as you read through these 8 chapters is that Liz's success isn't based on luck. It's based on a specific "publicity DNA"— a combination of relentless preparation, a keen understanding of the audience, and the ability to see connections that others miss. Liz's status as an award-winning PR professional was evident in how she mastered the media landscape for us. She often turned obstacles into opportunities for connection and growth.

The 2023 and 2024 eclipses were a historic success for *American Paper Optics*. We blew past our goals and stole the spotlight, evolving into a pulse point for the eclipse conversation happening across the United States. And to support our business goals, Liz Kelly worked closely with me and our team to produce record-breaking media visibility.

If you are considering this book, it's because you have a story that deserves a bigger stage. You aren't looking for a participation trophy; you're looking for the playbook that winners use to stay at the top. You have found it. Liz has distilled years of high-level experience into this PR guide that is as practical as it is inspiring.

Read this book, apply these 8 media boosters, and prepare yourself. Because when your "eclipse moment" arrives, you'll want to make sure that your brand's story is ready to shine.

PREFACE 

> When that moon is big and bright.
> It's a supernatural delight.
> Everybody's dancing in the moonlight.

–Dancing in the Moonlight by King Harvest

Have you ever had a career-changing moment that you took a time out to celebrate? After doing public relations for 20+ years, I've never seen the level of media results that our *Goody PR* agency got for *American Paper Optics (APO)* / Eclipse Glasses' National Publicity Campaign and Public Relations Campaign over a very short timeframe.

As a result, I wanted to celebrate this monumental moment in big ways, including writing this *Award-Winning Publicity* book to help you get top media coverage and gain value from positive press. I also think it's important for public relations professionals to take a day off to celebrate media wins, which I did for the 2024 Total Solar Eclipse.

Our *Goody PR* team was hired by *American Paper Optics* for 8.5 months primarily to get them earned media (TV, print, radio and podcasts) for their eclipse products. Their overall business goal was to sell 75 million eclipse glasses for the upcoming April 8, 2024, Total Solar Eclipse, and our main objective was to make them the go-to trusted brand.

Working closely with *APO's* CMO, Jason Lewin, and the digital marketing team, we secured record-breaking media coverage that included - TV interviews on every major network (*TODAY Show, CBS Saturday Morning, ABC Nightly News, NewsNation, Scripps News*) and coast-to-coast local TV, totaling 54 TV interviews.

And to provide you with some perspective, these epic publicity results are as rare as this Total Solar Eclipse —unless your story is at the center of breaking news.

On eclipse weekend, our client was still doing last minute TV interviews, which I supported remotely from my iPhone. *APO's* CEO, John Jerit, emphasized in one TV interview, **"You have to experience totality. It's going to be WILD!"**

After months of hearing about the importance of being on the direct path of the eclipse, I wanted to witness totality (best views with complete darkness) —especially since this type of eclipse would not happen again over the U.S. for another 20 years!

Fortunately, I was invited to join a group of 600 space geeks to watch this "Superbowl in the Sky" in Texas. One of the publicity campaign spokespeople, Astronomer, Hubble Space Telescope team and *Solar Snap* Inventor Dr. Doug Duncan organized this "Totality Over Texas" event.

Eclipse experts from *JPL-NASA* spoke there Friday–Sunday in Austin, Texas, where I had lunch with an Astronaut. And then Doug hosted an eclipse watch party on Monday, April 8, 2024, in the Texas Hill Country. Many speakers shared prayers and hopes for good weather on eclipse day because the forecast was not good.

As background, Doug invented *Solar Snap: The Eclipse App and Kit* to let you safely take epic eclipse photos with your smartphone. *APO* produces and sells this kit, and I set up many media interviews for Doug as part of this publicity campaign.

The anticipation for this April 8, 2024, Total Solar Eclipse moment was extraordinary for millions across the United States. Many people remembered the previous Total Solar Eclipse over the U.S. on August 21, 2017, that was watched by 216 million Americans.

Because of the bad weather forecast, I was not sure if traveling to Texas was the best move. However, Doug shared a theory with me that was hopeful. He explained that if we got really lucky the clouds would break right before the eclipse because the temperature usually drops.

During the campaign, many eclipse experts recommended "be mobile" and "be ready to change locations." I was determined to see this historic eclipse on the path of totality, so I called experts for last minute travel advice. I even booked a flight to Indianapolis. Jason (CMO) was going to the *Indianapolis Motor Speedway* because they bought 100,000 custom *APO* eclipse glasses for their watch party. I also considered going to Rochester, NY.

After much thought, I decided to stick to my Texas travel plan because I wanted to be with Doug's space geeks. Millions traveled to be on the direct path of totality with the longest totality times in the Texas Hill Country outside Austin and San Antonio. There were thousands of eclipse celebrations, millions of campers, and even weddings planned around this astronomical event.

Fortunately, I had a rent-a-car, and was mobile. I remember being so excited that I woke up at 5AM on eclipse morning at a Los Angeles friend's home. She lived about 60 minutes away from Doug's eclipse watch event at *Horseshoe Bay Resort*. I went for a walk with her around 6AM, and the sky was filled with dark clouds.

Based on Doug's weather prediction that the clouds might break right before the eclipse, I refused to give up hope. Horseshoe Bay was supposed to get 4 minutes and 17 seconds of totality at 1:34 PM CST. And when I checked different weather apps, there was a potential for 2 hours of "partly cloudy" there from 12-2PM. So I thanked our LA host, and headed to Horseshoe Bay.

During this early morning drive, I listened to our *Guardians of the Galaxy* Playlist on *Pandora*, and prayed for a miracle in the sky. Memorable lines from these top songs are quoted in the beginning of each chapter in this book for this reason.

There were road signs everywhere warning about major traffic jams. However, few cars were on the road, probably because of the ominous clouds.

When I arrived at *Horseshoe Bay Resort* around 8AM, Doug's guests were having breakfast on the lawn outside. Despite the gloom, our spirits were hopeful that Doug's forecast would come true.

I was wearing my lucky pink and purple scarf that I wore for the October 2023 Annular Eclipse in Albuquerque, New Mexico, about 6 months prior. For that Ring of Fire eclipse, clouds were also predicted. However, blue skies prevailed at the *International Balloon Fiesta* event where I watched this eclipse with 100k people and my team.

With telescopes out, Doug and *NASA* Scientists were ready to answer questions about the moon, sun and this historic Total Solar Eclipse.

When the totality time finally approached, the clouds magically started to break. You could feel the joy and relief in the people there. And sure enough, the sun came out by about 1 PM for the highly anticipated 1:34 PM totality experience. Many sat in chairs, but I joined friends lying flat on the grass for the perfect, straight-up view.

During totality, complete darkness took over the sky. The birds and bats flew over us in a flurry, thinking it was dusk. At first, we saw the diamond-ring effect, which happens at the beginning and end of a Total Solar Eclipse. And then I was beyond grateful to capture part of totality on video with my *iPhone*. Totality is the only time that you can look directly at an eclipse safely without wearing eclipse glasses or using camera filters.

After several hugs, thank yous and good-byes, I drove a few hours to the Austin airport later that day for the only flight I could get back to Los Angeles. During this drive, it poured rained. Thinking back on this totality experience and campaign, I smiled and gave thanks.

Our goal for this *Award-Winning Publicity* quick guide is to help you magnify your story with 8 Media Boosters. You can use these new strategies, media examples and reporter insights to propel your brand forward and boost your business results.

After using these public relations skills, I want you to also be singing; *Everybody's dancing in the moonlight.*

So buckle up, get your highlighter out, and start thinking creatively about how you can add the Story Magic of a Total Solar Eclipse to your publicity campaigns.

And P.S. - I am publishing this book now because there will be another Total Solar Eclipse this year on August 12, 2026. However, this eclipse will not be seen in the United States. Instead, you can travel to the path of totality, which will cross Greenland, Iceland, northern Spain, parts of Russia and a small section of Portugal.

INTRODUCTION 

We're so pleased to be with you (sky).
Look around see what you do (blue).
Everybody smiles at you.

–Mr. Blue Sky by Electric Light Orchestra

Are you a small business owner, CEO/Founder, CMO, Thought Leader, Marketing / Communications Director, Publicist, author, entrepreneur, and/or curious mind who wants to learn how to magnify your story with award-winning publicity?

If yes, this how-to-do public relations quick guide is designed to help you boost your brand and business results with earned media coverage (TV, print/digital, radio/podcasts and video) that is worth 3x the value of any paid ad.

Based on doing marketing and public relations campaigns for 20+ years primarily for small businesses, thought leaders and nonfiction authors who specialize in health, wellness, business, finance, leadership, technology and entertainment, you can learn our insider secrets that most PR agencies would never share.

To help you amplify your story, there are case studies, media examples, and proven strategies based on our *Goody PR* client campaigns and media expert interviews.

As background, this book was inspired by our Award-Winning Publicity Campaign and Public Relations Program for *American Paper Optics (APO)/* Eclipse Glasses. You will learn how this timely campaign exceeded all expectations.

Using our 8 Media Boosters, you also will learn how to secure national media coverage on the *TODAY Show, CNN, BBC World News, NewsNation, PBS, People Magazine, Forbes, Fast Company, NPR*, along with many local TV stations and top podcasts.

This book and every chapter is written using the power of threes, which is the most effective way to communicate and do media interviews. By sharing messages with three key points, you can have a much higher impact and better audience retention.

So let's start by reviewing the Top 3 Benefits for reading this book.

3 *Award-Winning Publicity* Book Benefits for Readers

PART 1: Build PR Success Strategy - To set you up for success, use our Story Magic and Creative Campaign Boosters as a roadmap.

PART 2: Gain Positive Press Value - Get free publicity and increase your credibility and sales using our 3Ms: Media Outreach, Media Training and Media Relations Boosters.

PART 3: Magnify and Measure Wins - Make your story go viral with Digital Marketing, Book Marketing and Top Media Boosters. Measure your media and business wins.

PLUS: **Bonus Content with reporter and expert insights.**

While it is not easy to get top earned media coverage, you can get feature stories about your brand with the right public relations strategy, unique media hooks, and gold standard practices.

So if you're ready to have the world fall in love with your brand, let us show you how you can attract more sales through a unique and inspiring story. You want to earn the respect of reporters so that they cover your story as "news" for no charge. This type of earned media coverage will increase your credibility and ultimately boost your business.

Overall, our Mission is to amplify your brand, business or book with Award-Winning Publicity that supports your overall goals, purpose and passion.

To get started, let's take a closer look at the 3 takeaways in this Introduction with more insights on how you can advance your story using these new strategies and examples.

Introduction: 3 Takeaways

1. **What is Award-Winning Publicity?**

2. **What's in this Award-Winning Publicity book?**

3. **Why Resilience is a Must for PR Campaigns?**

1. What is Award-Winning Publicity?

This how-to guide will teach you the secrets for getting award-winning publicity that is high impact, and ultimately goes viral.

Let's take a closer look at the definition and case study examples that can make your brand get noticed on a national stage. It's important to remember that local press can propel you into a national spotlight, so don't discount that coverage.

Award-Winning Publicity Definitions

1. Positive press that contributes to a clear and measurable impact on business goals.

2. Earned media coverage by a reporter that boosts a brand's positive sentiment through unique and emotional storytelling.

3. A strategic, creative campaign that breaks through the noise with social impact and receives third party validation.

While you might win a Publicity Campaign Award, People of the Year Award, Company Award, Book Award and/or Impact Award, you don't have to win an award to get award-winning publicity.

You can attract media wins by developing fresh, new story ideas that boost your emotional connections, trust and loyalty. One story can have a priceless impact.

And then if the stars line up right, your story might get a press award like this Upper Midwest Regional Emmy Award®.

Media Win: *PBS* Story wins *Regional Emmy Award* ®

To magnify your brand, a journalist may nominate a story about you for awards.

For example, I secured a feature interview with *Pioneer PBS* about the World War II book called *40 Thieves on Saipan* for Authors Joseph Tachovksy and Cynthia Kraack.

It took two years from the first pitch to the producer to *Pioneer PBS* winning an *Upper Midwest Region Emmy Award* ® for this 20-minute story in the Historical/Cultural/Nostalgic long-form content category.

The award-winning publicity process included every Media Booster in this book, including finding a unique story, media outreach, many follow-ups, media training, potential questions, curating their photos and videos, and then a half-day of filming.

You can read more about the backstory in the Media Relations Booster chapter. You can learn how our mantra, "be patient, persistent and never desperate with reporters" helped us get to the finish line.

* * *

Your challenge is defining and telling a Wow Story like this one that immediately gets a reporter to say, "Yes, I want to cover that story." To help you get there, this *Award-Winning Publicity* guide will teach you how.

Our Vision is to help 1 million small business owners, thought leaders and authors skyrocket their brand through the power of positive publicity.

And as part of this Introduction, here are the big picture differences between **Publicity versus Public Relations** to provide more context. Many people do not know the differences. You will see both of these terms throughout this book. And you need both to be successful in your marketing initiatives.

What is Publicity?	What is Public Relations?
Focus is on Media Outreach to get earned media coverage for free to generate public attention.	Focus is on a comprehensive public relations program with multiple elements, including publicity.
Publicity gets a brand in the headlines, and is one of the tactics for public relations.	Public relations is a strategic, long-term process for building and managing a brand's reputation and relationships.
A brand has no say in what the media says in stories, which can lead to positive or negative publicity.	Public relations seeks to curate messages that reach a desired target audience.

Bottom line, you need both a creative and timely Publicity Campaign as part of your overall Public Relations Program to succeed in your promotions journey. You will find insider tips and secrets for both in this how-to book.

2. What's in this *Award-Winning Publicity* book?

In this quick guide, you will learn 8 Media Boosters to magnify your story in short chapters for each step. Each booster is designed to help your brand take off like a rocket and rise above all the noise in your competitive landscape.

8 Media Booster Chapters

STEP 1: Story Magic Booster — Define Your Diamond Ring Effect

STEP 2: Creative Campaign Booster — Map Out Your Public Relations Strategies and Tactics

STEP 3: Media Outreach Booster — Develop Unique Story Hooks to Secure Top Media Coverage

STEP 4: Media Training Booster — Be a Superstar Media Spokesperson

STEP 5: Media Relations Booster — Build Long-term Relationships with Reporters

STEP 6: Digital Marketing Booster — Reach Millions with Online Strategy, Video and AI

STEP 7: Book Marketing Booster — Attract Media Before, During and After Publishing

STEP 8: Top Media Booster — Magnify, Measure and Make a Story Go Viral

This *Award-Winning Publicity* storytelling process is an art.

You can learn these unique marketing skills using the three sections and eight chapters:

Part 1: Build PR Success Strategy

The first two chapters of this book will set you up for publicity success.

Step 1: Story Magic Booster will teach you how to develop a Wow Story to get a reporter to say Yes, I want to cover your story.

Step 2: Creative Campaign Booster can help you build an innovative publicity campaign using proven strategics and tactics.

Part 2: Gain Positive Press Value

To help you gain meaningful media coverage, Part 2 focuses on the 3Ms: Media Outreach, Media Training and Media Relations to ensure long-term success.

Step 3: Media Outreach Booster will teach you how to find and send story ideas to the right reporters.

Once you secure an interview, **Step 4: Media Training Booster** can teach you how to be a Superstar Media Spokesperson. Based on our media coaching tips, you can learn how to be clear, concise and compelling. This chapter will cover what to say, along with on-camera tips for TV and radio/podcast interviews.

And in **Step 5: Media Relations Booster**, you will learn how to build long-term media relationships, so you get invited back. These reporter relationships are invaluable.

Part 3: Magnify and Measure Wins

Part 3 will provide you with extra media boosters to magnify and measure your wins.

Step 6: Digital Marketing Booster is filled with social media tips to better present your personal brand online. This chapter primarily highlights how to develop an overall strategy, use AI and produce videos that increase your engagement.

And if you have a book, **Step 7: Book Marketing Booster** uncovers how to maximize your book promotions Before, During and After launch. Writing a book is great way to add to your thought leadership brand. This detailed marketing checklist can also help anyone with a product to promote.

And the final chapter, **Step 8: Top Media Booster**, provides PR agency secrets for how to get national publicity, calculate results, and make your story go viral.

Using these new tools, case studies and reporter insights, you can shine a brighter light on your brand, business or book with award-winning publicity.

3. Why Resilience is a Must for PR Campaigns

While these 8 Media Boosters may sound easy, getting publicity can be very challenging. To be successful, you must be able to bounce back quickly from rejection. It is a process that will require you to be resilient and find inner strength when you get countless "Nos", or no response at all, from reporters.

You just can't take it personally every time you get a pass from a reporter. Instead, you must simply regroup and say "Next" or "Next time."

Your resilience skill is a muscle that you must build to truly thrive in public relations. You must believe that by failing forward, it can actually result in a better outcome.

To thrive in public relations, you cannot feel defeated by rejection by reporters. Ninety-nine percent of reporters will never tell you WHY they are passing on your story. You must accept these hurdles are just part of the publicity process.

Being fearless as a PR professional or expert spokesperson requires grit, determination, and perseverance.

The faster that you can let go of rejection, the sooner you will find a reporter who says Yes. Be resilient, and keep pitching your top media wish list until you get a YES.

Publicity Pro Tip: Fail Forward from Rejection with Resilience

How Failing Second Grade boosted Inner Strength

To find your willpower, think back at a life experience where you got rejected or failed forward. Was the long-term outcome more positive than expected?

Sometimes there is a good reason for a reporter's rejection, but you don't know why at the time. Maybe it will result in a better story later like our *TODAY Show* experience?

As an example, my life-changing event was failing second grade in a spectacular way. I had just transferred from a Catholic school to a private prep school. Everyone in my class had received their report cards – except me. So at 7 years old, I bravely marched down to the principal's office and asked, "Where are my report cards?"

The principal was very kind, and said, "We've been meaning to talk to you because we think you were not ready for second grade. You can either go back to first grade now, or repeat second grade." (And P.S., my report card was all Cs, Ds, and Fs.)

Without hesitation, I immediately decided to repeat second grade —at 7 years old. What I did not anticipate was how that decision would launch me into leadership roles throughout my twelve years at this school. As a sports team captain, class President, and tutor for other students, I excelled by this setback versus feeling defeated.

So what bumps have you overcome that gave you inner strength? And how can you use your courage to be even more fearless with your publicity campaigns?

To help you better understand how our *Award-Winning Publicity* best practices work, you will find many case studies and media examples to encourage you to never give up like this one:

Media Example: Tears of Joy on *TODAY Show* Set

I wrote *Award-Winning Publicity* to help you get media wins and feel the same joy that I felt on the *TODAY Show* set for our *Goody PR* client after a temporary setback.

While standing on the sidelines in Studio 1A in Rockefeller Center in New York City, I literally became teary for our client, *Warriors Heart.*

Watching this story LIVE on set was surreal. It was the result of ten months of pitching the producers with a lot of input from the *Warriors Heart* team and two Superstar Media Spokespeople.

After months of pitching and planning, this interview was cancelled at the last minute in December. After regrouping, I re-pitched *Warriors Heart* with a different media hook for February. Fortunately, this national interview was rescheduled, and had an even better result.

The guests were very passionate about sharing their personal recovery stories and *Warriors Heart's* mission to help military, veterans and first responders struggling with addiction, PTSD and co-occurring issues.

During this inspiring segment, a *Warriors Heart* alumnus and Green Beret (ret) Ted Lanier openly shared how he overcame a 17-year opiate addiction. He encouraged others struggling to seek help. Warriors Heart's Clinical Director Vonnie Nealon also appeared in this segment. Ted praised Vonnie for "saving his life."

Behind-the-scenes, I provided media training for these spokespeople who had both never done a TV interview. While they did not rehearse a script, we practiced answering potential questions. You can learn more about our Media Training tips in Step 4.

And fortunately, this 7.5-minute TV coverage was worth over $863,000+ in Calculated Publicity Value and reached 4+ million people, according to a *Nielsen Media Report.*

One of the most important things that you must do is embrace your topic with passion before you start pitching reporters. As a publicist or thought leader, you should LOVE to learn and research as I did for *Warriors Heart* for 10 years.

And to give you new ideas, I will share the winning strategy, data and results behind our *American Paper Optics* / Eclipse Glasses campaign. Fortunately, *Goody PR* won six PR industry awards (three Winners and three Finalists), and I will explain what worked best.

Your mission, if you choose to accept, is to be open to learning and applying these new strategies and skills to transport your brand forward.

And if you decide to hire a PR agency versus doing-it-yourself, this guide can provide you with invaluable insights to be a better collaborator and partner.

As a side note, if you choose to hire a PR agency, you don't need to spend $15,000 — $20,000/month to get award-winning publicity results. You can hire our *Goody PR* agency or another boutique agency who can get you high impact results for a much lower investment.

So are you ready to start winning hearts and minds, build credibility and trust, and gain loyal customers by applying these new publicity skills?

If yes, keep reading with a highlighter, take notes, and embrace brainstorming so you can come up with creative media hook ideas that are unique, timely and relevant.

And by combining these 8 *Award-Winning Publicity* boosters, tools and strategies, your personal and/or business brand can become unstoppable.

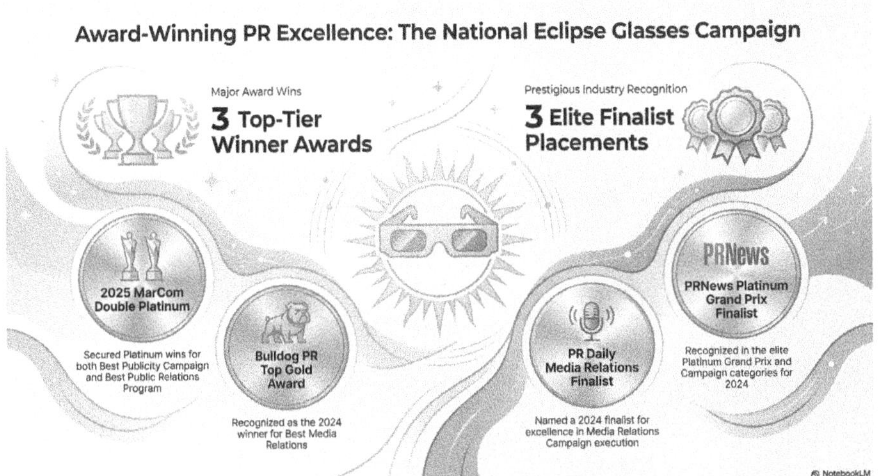

BUILD PR SUCCESS STRATEGY

To set you up for success, use our Story Magic and Creative Campaign Boosters as a roadmap.

STORY MAGIC BOOSTER:
Define Your Diamond Ring Effect

Ho, Ho, Ho, It's Magic,
You Know, Never Believe It's Not So.

–*Magic* by Pilot

Can you explain your story magic in a Wow Story in 1-2 sentences to get a top reporter to say YES, I want to cover that story? You built a great company, product and/or wrote an awesome book, but how do you get the media to care?

The fastest way to get earned media coverage for free is to pitch a Wow Story with something surprising that makes the reporter look twice. This magic is what makes your story become a watercooler topic that people discuss way beyond your interview.

Instead of pitching a reporter a story about "how great you are," propose a unique story that your competition cannot tell. And emphasize how your insights can educate, entertain and/or connect with their audience.

To help you get started with this Step 1, here are 3 Story Magic Boosters to strengthen your chances of getting top media coverage:

STEP 1: Story Magic Boosters

1.1 Define Your Diamond Ring Effect

1.2 Emotionally Connect with a Powerful Backstory

1.3 Research Trends and Competition to Define Your Uniqueness

So are you ready to define what I often call your "Media Gold"? It's not easy to find a story that is rare and unique. Your media hook must stand out in a sea of thousands of fantastic pitches reporters get every day.

Your top skill for this Media Booster is brainstorming. I've often said that I want to get a *Goody PR* t-shirt that says, "Always Brainstorming" because it's what we LOVE to do.

Let's take a closer look at these Story Magic Boosters and examples:

1.1 Define Your Diamond Ring Effect

You must work hard to define your story magic, which includes the aha moment that someone feels looking at the diamond ring effect during a Total Solar Eclipse. This process can require you to take a lot of walks, schedule strategy calls, and test out different approaches to see what gets you the most interest from reporters.

Defining your story magic will not always be obvious.

Changing one sentence or word can give a new twist to your pitch.

Similar to the eclipse magic in the sky that almost 700 million people viewed in the U.S. on April 8, 2024, as either a Total Solar Eclipse (44 million) or Partial Eclipse (652 million), you want your brand to stand out and sparkle.

The diamond ring effect phenomenon happens at the beginning and end of a Total Solar Eclipse. It is a spectacular burst of light that appears on one side of the ring around the moon by the sun that makes it look like a diamond ring.

During our Total Solar Eclipse experience on the direct path of totality in the Texas Hill Country, everyone cheered for this dazzling jewel. Search online for "Diamond Ring Effect" to see photographs, and watch these videos to hear the joyful reactions.

The best media stories ignite emotions. So think about what story magic can you share that will move the audience? Your story must be memorable. Long after your interview is published, you want people to keep re-sharing your story.

So what is your Wow Story that will make people look twice?

Why You Need to Brainstorm Your Story Magic Ideas

If you do a *Google* search to find out how many other companies are experts are in your field, you might be blown away by your competition to get positive publicity.

So when you define your media gold, think about the personal stories behind each spokesperson that are unique to that individual. It could be related to the positive impact made by your CEO/Founder and/or anyone on your team and/or a comeback story.

For every *Goody PR* client, our team regularly brainstorms ideas with them to better define each pitch. If you have the right story at the right time with the right spokesperson, the stars can line up much faster for you to get positive press.

To illustrate the power of a unique story, here is a case study example:

Defining Story Magic for Eclipse Glasses Publicity Campaign

To define *American Paper Optics/* Eclipse Glasses story magic, I came up with ten unique media hooks with the core team. You will learn more about how to develop powerful topics in the Step 3: Media Outreach Booster chapter.

As background, our client's primary goal was to raise awareness of their "Made in the U.S.A." products and become the go-to trusted brand for consumers. Their products included a variety of eclipse glasses, maps, t-shirts, hats, books, *MoonPies, Solar Snap: The Eclipse App and Kit*, and more.

While many of their media stories focused on educating the public about why you MUST wear eclipse glasses to safely view an eclipse, I was always brainstorming new ideas.

Many story pitches were about *APO's* custom eclipse glasses and events hosted by major organizations. For example, *NASA* donated 2.1 million custom eclipse glasses made by *APO* to events, including 80,000 for the 2023 *Albuquerque International Balloon Fiesta* alone. In addition, *Warby Parker* gave away 500k custom eclipse glasses made by *APO* at their stores nationwide.

While each of these custom glasses orders had a unique backstory, one media hook had a more personal story that really stood out.

Media Example: *KENS5 CBS San Antonio*

Diamond Ring Effect Eclipse Wedding Glasses

As a Story Magic Booster example, one of our favorite eclipse stories was about a diamond ring effect eclipse wedding. Fortunately, the couple was getting married in San Antonio, Texas, and *KENS5 CBS San Antonio* covered it at the last minute.

APO explained to me that the scientist couple designed custom diamond ring effect eclipse glasses for their 2024 Total Solar Eclipse weekend wedding.

The bride and groom traveled with friends to San Antonio from California to be on the path of totality to get the best views. The happy couple and many of their guests were Astrophysicists, who study celestial objects like galaxies, stars, planets and black holes. This backstory added to their overall Wow Story.

Throughout the campaign, I was pitching a lot of different ideas to *KENS5 CBS* because San Antonio was on the direct path of totality. Nothing interested them —until this eclipse wedding pitch that got immediate approval and coverage.

Because this couple's story was unique and timely, the anchor jumped at the opportunity. And because it was the Friday before the big eclipse on Monday, the reporter drove the same day directly to the rehearsal at the church.

The bride was our main media contact and spokesperson. And everyone involved in this eclipse wedding was passionate about sharing this heart-warming story.

The main story visual was the couple's custom diamond ring effect eclipse glasses. Everyone wore them during the segment, which made the coverage even more spectacular.

And while this story was not focused on *American Paper Optics*, it cross-marketed them as the eclipse glasses manufacturer with a link to their website in the online story.

* * *

So what is your unique story magic? And what visuals can you use to amplify your message?

1.2 Emotionally Connect with a Powerful Backstory

To emotionally connect with an audience, your personal backstory is your most powerful asset. Reporters love to cover stories that make their audience feel inspired, cheer, cry, scream, take action and/or laugh out loud.

To find this story magic, I often interview clients for over an hour about their personal and business WHY. While an hour may sound like a long time, it can take a while to find your media gold because it is a discovery process.

When I did public relations for my first book that featured dating tips, I remember reporters interviewing me for an hour for publications such as *The Washington Post* and *Christian Science Monitor*. Afterwards, I was quoted in only a few paragraphs. What I did not understand was that the reporter was digging for impactful soundbites that were unique and memorable.

If you're interviewed LIVE on TV or a top radio show for 2-5 minutes, you don't have that discovery time luxury. As a result, reporters want to see that you've already defined your story in a clear, concise and compelling way.

To uncover the story magic, ask yourself or your spokesperson these questions:

3 Personal Story Magic Questions

1. What was the aha moment that inspired you to launch your company, product or book?

2. What are 3 ways your insights can help others improve their health, finances, impact and/or other life skills?

3. What is your most important advice tip or message for the audience?

Sometimes it helps to go way back and think about what happened to you as a child to find a fresh new idea to pitch. For example, one of our former CEO clients is an entrepreneur. After his publicity campaign started, I discovered that he started a business selling recycled golf balls from the local golf course at 8 years old. This entrepreneurial story was unique with priceless visuals.

While many think this discovery process is easy, give yourself a break. Recognize that it can take time to define how your unique story or product can help others. The feelings that you want to convey may not be obvious at first.

Your story magic may also be connected to a life-changing or current event. Let's take a closer look at an example of a story that emotionally connected on many levels.

Media Examples: *PBS* and *KTLA*
How Palisades Fire Survivor Story Moved Audiences

Physician, researcher and *Common Wisdom* Author Dr. Laura Gabayan already had a heartfelt backstory about her life-changing health challenges. When she lost her home of 18 years in the historic 2025 Palisades Fire in Los Angeles, it took her backstory to another level.

To help others, Dr. Gabayan interviewed people who were considered "wise" to uncover what makes someone think outside-the-box to solve problems. As a former ER doctor, she was frustrated by textbook answers from doctors that were not helping her get better. She wanted to discover what makes people think differently.

As a result of her wisdom study, Dr. Gabayan scientifically identified 8 life skills that contribute to wisdom, including Resilience, Kindness, Positivity, Spirituality, Humility, Tolerance, Creativity and Curiosity (in that order of importance).

While this media hook worked great when the *Common Wisdom* book first launched, the tragic loss of her home in the Palisades Fire provided new and timely insights.

It also made her story relevant because it was connected to headline news. There were sadly 16,000+ structures burned and 31 lives lost in the Palisades Fire and Eaton Fire with millions impacted.

As a result, Dr. Gabayan was interviewed by a national *PBS* show and *KTLA* (top Los Angeles station). She was also asked to be a featured speaker at a local wellness conference.

To help others facing major life obstacles like this fire, Dr. Gabayan shared how her top three wisdom skills (Resilience, Positivity and Kindness) gave her the inner strength to rebuild emotionally.

During her *KTLA* interview, Dr. Gabayan started by sharing that during the first week after the fire all she did was cry. She then expanded by reflecting on how her wisdom skills helped her be resilient and remain positive.

To add powerful visuals, we provided photos and video of her home that sadly burned. The devastation looked like a war zone. During her *PBS* interview, Dr. Gabayan emphasized that she not only lost her home, but her community as well.

And while her wedding photos were lost in the fire, she shared digital images on *KTLA* that her wedding photographer found. These images were priceless.

* * *

Your Story Magic Challenge is to both Educate and Entertain

Along with emotionally connecting, your Wow Story should entertain and educate the audience. So step back and brainstorm how your life story can offer new insights.

Think about your personal WHY, backstory, goals and desire to make a positive impact —and then ask, why does it matter today? And how are your tips different from others?

> **Story Magic Example: *KFMB CBS8* and *CW* San Diego**
>
> **Writers behind *Oscar & GRAMMY* Award Winners Never Gave Up**

Sometimes you have to delve into your past to find a unique story that can both entertain and educate an audience. Fortunately, I found this type of media hook that was covered by *KFMB CBS8* and *CW* in San Diego, California. It was for their *Zevely Zone* segment that celebrates local heroes and good news.

The media hook that got the host to approve it was **How 2 Writers behind *Oscars* and *GRAMMYs* Never Gave Up** —with writer tips for how to get your work published.

Getting this story approved was not easy. Our client Rick Bleiweiss was a *GRAMMY* Nominated Producer and *Blackstone Publishing*

VP of Business Development, who did not live in San Diego. He had written a new mystery book, *Pigeon Scorbion & The Barbershop Detectives*, but there was no local connection or wow factor.

So I brainstormed with Rick to find a local hero to include in the pitch. Fortunately, Rick had recently published a new mystery book, *The Archivist*, by Rex Pickett, who lived in San Diego. And because Rex's popular book was behind the blockbuster movie *Sideways*, we had a local hero with star power. And P.S., the Director of *Sideways* won the *Oscar* for Best Adapted Screenplay.

While the host Jeff Zevely did mention their two new mystery books, the focus was really about the authors' backstories and writing advice tips to never give up.

For visuals, Rick provided photos of some of the biggest names in the music industry, whom he produced. These photos included Rick with his clients Pink, Alicia Keys, Kiss, the Bee Gees, U2, Melissa Etheridge, and the Backstreet Boys.

Rex also described being on the *Sideways* movie set, and provided images of Actors Paul Giamatti, Thomas Hayden Church, and Virginia Madsen.

Overall, this 4-minute story aired 5 times (20 minutes total airtime) on the local *CBS* and *CW*.

And because San Diego is ranked as the 30th largest media market or DMA out of 210 U.S. media markets, the overall Calculated Publicity Value was over $51,000, according to a *Nielsen Media Report*.

So think about how your story can both entertain and educate, and get a producer to say YES.

1.3 Research Trends and Competition to Define Your Uniqueness

Another major part of strengthening your Story Magic Booster is to research the current headlines, trends and competition. You want to identify how your business, brand or product is timely, relevant and unique —and it all starts with a story.

Remember, there is a ton of competition for TV interviews, radio airtime and print space related to your topic. With millions of doctors, lawyers, CEOs, entrepreneurs, thought leaders, and authors all trying to reach the same reporters, you must stand out.

Of course, everyone wants to be on the top media, but it's just not that easy to get a green light for your story. And keep-in-mind, it's 100 times harder to get a Yes if you are not a celebrity.

As a result, you must spend hours researching trends and statistics that can make your story important to share NOW. See what reporters are already covering today related to your topic, and then identify how you can provide a new twist or insights.

Your Thought Leader Competition for Media Interviews

To provide more context on why research is so important before pitching the media, here is expanded data on the competitive landscape. There are hundreds, if not millions, of experts who do what you do, so how are you different?

1+ million Doctors in the U.S. —There are 1,044,734 licensed physicians in the U.S. and District of Columbia. This physician workforce is 23 percent larger than in 2010, according to the *FSMB Census of Licensed Physicians in the United States, 2022.*

1.3 million Lawyers in the U.S. —There are over 1.3 million lawyers in the United States, with the *American Bar Association* reporting 1,322,649 active lawyers as of January 1, 2024.

34 Million Small Businesses (50-1500 employees) in the U.S. —Small businesses account for 99 percent of all business in the United States, according to the U.S. *Small Business Association* (SBA).

44 Million books on *Amazon* —While it is hard to find the exact number of books published on *Amazon*, it is estimated to be over 44 million in 2025. And according to *Book Writer Pros,* "On *Amazon Kindle Direct Publishing* (KDP), approximately 7,500 new Kindle eBooks are published daily. This translates to around 225,000 eBooks monthly and about 2.7 million eBooks annually."

So every time you pitch a reporter, do your homework first, create a compelling story – and remember, don't get upset by rejections or no response.

For every pitch to producers, you want to get to the point immediately with a catchy headline. Researching what similar experts are currently saying in news stories is a great way to identify timely trends and ways to differentiate your pitch.

To help you find your story magic, here are three easy ways to research trends:

3 Media Pitch Research Tips

1. **Read Related Headline News** —Search your topic on *Google*, and then click the *NEWS* tab. Pay careful attention to the publication dates and topics for the latest news related to your industry and specialty. Find a way to connect your story to headlines.

2. **Set up *Google Alerts* for Your Topic(s)** —Another way to stay informed about what people are talking about is to set up daily *Google Alerts* for your topic(s). For example, you may learn there is a new study related to your expertise that you can discuss. You can also identify top reporters covering your subject. If a reporter is already writing about your industry, they are much more likely to be interested in a new perspective.

3. **Search Keyword Phrases and Find Relevant Data** — Reporters love it when you can provide them with relevant data and numbers from reliable sources. So if you are looking for a specific statistic, search using keyword phrases with quotes around them. For example, you might search on "autism numbers in the U.S." to find current statistics.

   Many media organizations even hire Data Journalists to find and analyze relevant statistics. The more reliable information that you can provide producers to back up your pitch, the more you increase your chances of getting earned media.

Let's take a closer look at a thought leader and author who obtained a top media interview. Her unique media hook stood out among other parenting experts.

> **Story Magic Example:** *FOX 29 Philadelphia*
> **How Parents can be Best Friends with Their Teens**

To promote the new book *Raising Good Humans Every Day* by Mindfulness Mama Mentor and Number 1 Bestselling Author, Hunter Clarke-Fields, I researched trends on parenting. Because most parents struggle raising kids during their teenage years, it seemed unique that Hunter was best friends with her two teenage daughters.

When researching this topic, I discovered that *Psychology Today* reports that 43 percent of parents wish to be best friends with their teens. This statistic showed there was a strong interest in tips for how to build stronger relationships with teens.

So the pitch was **How Parents can be Best Friends with Their Teens** — using Mindful Parenting Tips in Hunter's new book to *FOX 29 Philadelphia*. There was also a local connection because the author lived nearby in Delaware.

Not only did the producers LOVE this interview idea, they researched movie scene examples of mothers in conflict with teen daughter characters. The producers then asked if Hunter could give parenting advice tips after playing each video clip.

One of these movie examples included Jamie Lee Curtis (playing the mom) and Lindsay Lohan (playing her teenage daughter) having an argument in the popular film *Freaky Friday*.

This LIVE segment included a teaser promotion and interview with two anchors at the desk. The total air time was over eight minutes during their top morning show.

And because Philadelphia is the 5th largest media market in the United States, this one TV interview was worth a **Calculated Publicity Value of $40,240, according to a *Nielsen Media Report*.**

As another example about the importance of researching statistics, you always want to look for relevant studies. And if you find a new study related to your topic, you can pitch that your experts can comment on the results as a news story.

> **Timely Media Example: How a *Google Alert* turned into Media Coverage**
>
> **Veteran Health Experts weigh in on New Veteran Suicide Study**

As an example of how a *Google Alert* turned into a timely media story, let's look at how learning about a new veteran suicide study resulted in a *KSAT ABC News* San Antonio feature.

In our daily alerts, I discovered a new study by *Brown University's Cost of War Project* in 2021 that showed that more post-9/11 veterans sadly died by suicide than in combat. The study reported an estimate of 30,000 veteran suicides versus about 7,000 combat deaths during the same timeframe.

When I pitched reporters that *Warriors Heart* could provide veteran insights on this study, I added that their mission was to reduce the alarming average of 22 veteran suicides per day in the U.S. As a result, this story was approved almost immediately by this top local TV news station.

As a private and accredited residential treatment program exclusively for military, veterans and first responders, *Warriors Heart* had a powerful spokesperson. He was part of their recovery program team, a U.S. veteran, and had been in combat in Iraq.

* ❋ *

To help you review what you've learned, here are three Story Magic Booster Action Items. Each summary point includes publicity steps to propel your story into the spotlight.

STEP 1: Your Story Magic Booster Action Items Recap

As you wrap up this first chapter, look at your notes and determine your next steps for these 3 Story Magic Action Items. You can boost your brand and media results by applying these new skills.

1.1 Define Your Diamond Ring Effect

Go on walks, schedule a brainstorming call with your team, and then identify a unique Wow Story. Find powerful photos and/or b-roll video that can add to your story as visuals.

1.2 Emotionally Connect with a Powerful Backstory

Find an inspiring story that can entertain, educate and emotionally connect with your audience. Go back to your childhood or identify current events related to your story. Define what makes your story unique —with helpful tips and examples.

1.3 Research Trends and Competition to Define Your Uniqueness

Research relevant news stories and studies that connect to your story. Search for key statistics from reliable sources to support your pitch. And set up *Google Alerts* for your topic(s) to discover the latest headlines.

You always want to define your Wow Story with a Diamond Ring Effect, to be both memorable and have a positive impact.

If you can master this story magic skill, your publicity and business results can skyrocket. Always be brainstorming, do your research, and get ready to come up with a creative campaign in the next chapter.

CREATIVE CAMPAIGN BOOSTER: 
Map Out Your PR Strategies and Tactics

> Come and get your love,
> come and get your love,
> come and get your love now.
>
> *–Come and Get Your Love Now* by Redbone

Did you know that the *Guardians of the Galaxy* movie includes a Star-Lord's initial dance to the song *Come and Get Your Love Now* by *Redbone* that signified that he was about to start a journey? When you start planning your public relations initiatives, you need to develop a Creative Campaign as a success roadmap.

Use these Creative Campaign Boosters to outline your Public Relations Program that includes multiple elements. You want to document your goals, strategies, tactics and a campaign calendar. Your ultimate goal is to find innovative ways to attract media and get people to fall in love with your brand.

Instead of randomly pitching ideas to reporters, a campaign provides a comprehensive strategy with an overall theme for you and your team. In your plan, identify multiple ways to connect with your audience, including earned media, digital media, events, contests, promotions, partnerships and more.

Developing a campaign is meant to be a fun and innovative process. And if it helps, listen to music that makes you want to dance to boost your imagination.

And as a baseline, use the three Creative Campaign Boosters to increase your positive impact on the world.

STEP 2: Creative Campaign Boosters

2.1 Define Your Campaign Goals, Objectives and Budget

2.2 Identify Strategies and Tactics

2.3 Develop Your PR Program Campaign Calendar

Remember, you have a ton of competition, so dig deep to find new ways to magnify your story magic. You want to create a unique campaign theme that is supported by multiple strategies and tactics. To brainstorm, consider writing down potential headlines for news stories about your business, product or service.

Evaluate which one of these headlines you like best, and then prioritize ideas that are mostly likely to attract media coverage.

You're putting together a master campaign project plan, and there are many pieces that need to come together to produce business and media results.

So let's take a closer look at each of these Creative Campaign Boosters:

2.1 Define Your Campaign Goals, Objectives and Budget

As a first step, start by defining your overall PR campaign goals, objectives and budget. To get you started, let's review some broad definitions for this action item.

A PR plan should always start with clear and measurable goals. To do this step, you want to establish goals and ways to measure results. Based on input from the team, draft the big picture objectives for everyone to review and provide feedback.

Your PR Goals are your long-term desired outcomes.

Your PR Campaign Objectives should be SMART with specific measurements.

Write down your SMART Goals on a board for the team to review. These goals are Specific, Measurable, Attainable, Relevant and Time-bound and provide a framework.

Campaign Objective Example: Our campaign objective is to increase revenue by 20 percent within six months by promoting our new service through earned media.

Define Your PR Budget: Your overall budget will impact both the scope and impact of your Public Relations Program and Publicity Campaign. Money should always be put aside as part of your overall marketing budget to support your brand, business or book promotions. Without a budget, your impact will be limited to your individual efforts.

3 Budgets for Your Public Relations Program

Ideally, your PR budget should include these three elements:

1. **Marketing Budget** for brand messaging and voice, creative graphics, media giveaways, influencer marketing, travel, events and more.

2. **Digital Marketing Budget** for your website, social media, video and AI production, professional photos, and ad campaigns.

3. **Public Relations Budget** for publicity experts, press releases, software tools, partnerships, events, conferences, speaking, travel, awards submissions, and more.

If you are promoting a brand, your budget is a balancing act between the time, money and resources available to support your overall objectives.

As a long-term budget strategy, *Goody PR* has been fortunate to work with small business clients who made our monthly retainer fee part of their overall operating budget for 5+ and 10+ years. Because of their business models, these on-going publicity campaigns had long-term positive impacts on their bottom line results.

In other cases, I've done short-term contracts for 6-18 months that support a more focused campaign. This book will feature the *APO* eclipse glasses campaign that falls into this short-term category, along with long-term examples.

And if you have no PR budget, but a lot of time, you can always do the heavy lifting yourself by using the steps in this how-to book. I wrote this book for many reasons, including helping people who don't have funds to hire a public relations agency.

Yes, there are always ways to save money on a campaign. To be truly successful, you want to invest in hiring professionals who are experts in different areas to champion your campaign.

Please don't skip these Creative Campaign Booster planning steps. If your foundation is not solid, millions of dollars could be lost.

Goals Example 1: Sirius XM Radio Campaign had No Clear Objectives

When I worked for Myspace during its popularity peak, I remember being asked to step into a leadership role overnight to get a major marketing campaign back on track. They had a budget, but no one was actively managing the overall plan.

At the time, I was a Marketing/Project Manager contractor. However, Myspace told *Sirius/ XM Radio* that I was a Director being assigned to the project. The client had lost confidence that their $1.8 million integrated marketing campaign was on track, and my job was to work with the team to literally save this account.

When I was given 48 hours to prepare for a strategy meeting and fly from Los Angeles to Washington D.C. to meet with the *Sirius/ XM Radio* senior marketing team, I had to move at warp speed.

Members of the Myspace team told me that there were over 800 emails for this campaign already. It would be impossible to learn everything that fast. And despite all of this communication, the client did not believe that Myspace could deliver their project on time and on schedule.

When I stepped back and asked questions, I learned that there were no campaign objectives, goals or status reports. The target market had not been defined. In other words, no one was steering the ship.

After an emergency meeting with key stakeholders from both companies in Washington D.C., I worked with the internal Myspace team to clearly define these elements and put together a project dashboard report. This executive summary included color codes with red-, yellow-, and green- light icons to show which pieces were on schedule versus off-track.

By providing this big picture view to the *Sirius/XM Radio's* senior marketing team, the account was saved. And it was all because the client could finally see where the project was going. It was a fun campaign that centered around a Hip-Hop contest with many elements, including an *American Idol* style competition for the finalists in Las Vegas. Everyone was very happy at that finale after a successful campaign.

Fast forward to our more recent eclipse glasses campaign for *American Paper Optics*, I was fortunate to work with *APO's* CMO and the digital marketing team from *Bazztiki Digital* to develop campaign goals and objectives upfront.

Goals Example 2: *American Paper Optics* for Total Solar Eclipse Campaign

The big picture goal of *Goody PR's American Paper Optics/* Eclipse Glasses.com Public Relations Campaign (8.5 months, 8/15/23 – 4/30/24) was to promote *APO* through positive publicity as the Number 1 manufacturer of eclipse glasses.

Based on this big picture framework and strategy sessions, below were the award-winning campaign goals and objectives for this marketing initiative.

APO Campaign Objectives were more specific SMART Goals:

1. To increase public awareness, trust and credibility for *APO's* "Made in the U.S.A." eclipse glasses and products for the upcoming 2023 and 2024 eclipses.

2. To support *APO's* overall business goal to sell 75 million eclipse glasses (vs. 45 million in 2017) with national and local press coverage.

3. To give back by promoting *APO's* custom "Eclipse Glasses for a Cause" charity campaign. These eclipse glasses raised money and awareness for the *ALS Association* and *St. Jude's Children Research Hospital*.

* * *

The overall campaign project timeline included two phases:

Phase 1: Annular Eclipse/ "Ring of Fire" (Oct 14, 2023) —While Annular Eclipses happen a lot more often, our goal was to make this "Warm-Up Act" eclipse a big media event to build buzz leading up to the 2024 Total Solar Eclipse.

Phase 2: Total Solar Eclipse/ Great North American Eclipse (April 8, 2024) —This major celestial event will not happen again over the U.S. for 20 years (Aug 2044). Our primary focus for *APO's* Public Relations Program was to draw attention and sales for their ISO-certified eclipse glasses and products in sync with this historic celestial event.

To be more focused on our Media Outreach, we also defined their ideal target audience.

While *APO* had already received millions of custom orders from B2B (business-to-business) customers (Cleveland's *Rock and Roll Hall of Fame*, *The Perot Museum of Nature and Science*, and many more), our primary goal was to educate the B2C (business-to-consumer) market, which included:

Target Market: Consumers in all 48 U.S. adjacent states where both eclipses could be seen were the main target audience for this Public Relations Program.

For the 2024 Total Solar Eclipse, also called the *Great North American Eclipse*, approximately 44 million people lived on the path of totality, which included 15 U.S. States, 6 Canadian provinces and Mexico.

While this target market was a very broad audience, all ages wanted to see the eclipse.

For example, *Bill Nye the Science Guy* was stressing that kids of all ages should watch this monumental eclipse. Because the April 8th eclipse was on a Monday, many schools and universities closed and/or hosted events.

In addition, my mother's senior living community was planning a watch party. *APO* sent them eclipse glasses as a gift, and they loved watching the Total Solar Eclipse.

So step back and start documenting your overall publicity plan with campaign goals, objectives, budget, and target market.

2.2 Identify Strategies and Tactics

Your next step is to identify your Strategies and Tactics for your campaign to maximize your impact and bottom-line business results. While there is some overlap in the goals previously discussed, it's important to identify specific elements behind an award-winning publicity campaign to ensure success.

What are PR Strategies vs. Tactics?

From a big picture perspective, here is the difference between Strategies and Tactics for your Public Relations Program:

Strategies include your WHAT and WHY —The strategies include the overall messaging, setting goals and defining how the campaign results will be measured.

Tactics are the HOW —The tactics are your specific action items and tools that can support the overall campaign objectives. If they are not producing results, tactics should be reviewed often and adjusted to find a better approach.

While this section focuses on *APO's* campaign as a case study, you will also find our Top 10 Influencer Marketing Planning Tips at the end of this section. These high-impact tactic insights are Bonus Content based on our research.

So are you ready to dive into the detail behind this creative campaign?

PR Strategy Example: *APO* / Eclipse Glasses Campaign

Goody PR's American Paper Optics/ Eclipse Glasses Public Relations Program used several strategies and tactics to help them meet their overall business goal to sell 75 million eclipse glasses for the two 2023 and 2024 eclipses.

To ensure success, weekly meetings were held with key stakeholders.

Goody PR also sent Monthly Summary Reports with media coverage, airtime and the Total Reach for TV, print, radio, and podcast interviews. This report was sent to *APO's* senior leadership team (CEO, CMO and COO) and the digital marketing team. This executive summary helped everyone track media results and share their press online.

From a 30,000 foot view, here is an Infographic created by *NotebookLM* that is based on our recap video called: *3 Award-Winning PR Strategies*. This image summarizes the strategies behind this record-breaking campaign discussed in this chapter.

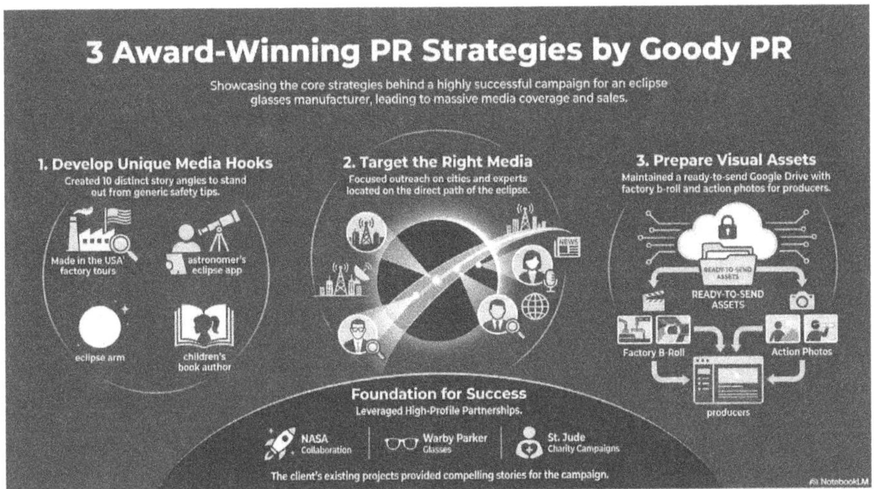

PR Strategies - Identify Your WHAT and WHY

To give you ideas for how to build a PR plan, *APO's* publicity campaign strategies included:

1. **Extensive Eclipse Research** —To prepare for this campaign, I read books about the history of eclipses, reviewed stories by eclipse experts, interviewed *APO's* eclipse experts and spokespeople, watched videos, attended webinars, and asked a lot of questions.

2. **Identified *APO's* Core Messaging** —For pitches, our team consistently emphasized that *APO* eclipse glasses were "Made in America" at a US-based factory, ISO-Certified, and recommended by the *American Astronomical Society/AAS* (third party validation).

3. **Created Unique Media Hooks** —To maximize media results, I developed ten unique, timely and relevant media hooks with the *APO* CMO and team. We also identified five main spokespeople with backstories to maximize positive publicity.

These media hooks will be described in detail in the next chapter, Media Outreach Booster.

4. **Compiled Digital Press Kits with Visuals Ready** —To provide consistent branding to tell *APO's* story, our team created multiple digital press kits for each key product on *Google Drives*. For example, there was a *Google Drive* with photos and b-roll videos for eclipse glasses, and another one for *Solar Snap The Eclipse App and Kit*. These drives allowed us to be ready for last-minute media interviews with approved images.

PR Tactics – Identify Your HOW

To explain the HOW we magnified this story, here is a list of our *APO* PR Campaign Tactics:

1. **Wrote and Distributed Monthly Press Releases** —To boost *APO's* SEO (Search Engine Optimization) and raise awareness of their eclipse glasses products, we sent out monthly press releases that linked to their website, online store and videos. These press releases often were re-published in 200+ media outlets coast-to-coast.

2. **Targeted National and Local Reporters** —For this campaign, *Goody PR* did extensive research to identify both national and local media in cities on the two eclipse paths. These reporters were most likely to cover eclipse glasses stories based on their location, job title and previous coverage.

3. **Developed Custom *Google Alerts*** —To identify reporters more interested in eclipses, *Goody PR* followed press coverage for specific topics. For example, *APO* made 100k custom eclipse glasses for *The University of Texas at Austin*, which was covered by *KXAN NBC Austin*. Because this city was on the direct path of totality, these *Google Alerts* helped us identify the best reporters to contact. Our *APO* coverage included seven media interviews in the San Antonio-Austin area alone.

4. **Developed "Eclipse Glasses for a Cause" Holiday Giving Campaign** - During the holiday season 2023, there was a lull in

coverage in-between the two eclipse events. To highlight how *APO* was giving back, the team created an "Eclipse Glasses for a Cause" campaign. This social impact story highlighted how *APO* created two custom charity eclipse glasses to benefit *St Jude's Research Hospital for Children* and the *ALS Association*. This campaign had personal connections to *APO's* COO/CFO, and was covered by local TV.

5. **Developed Annular Eclipse Event Promotions for Media VIPs** - To magnify the October 2023 Annular Eclipse, our *Goody PR* team attended the *Albuquerque/ABQ International Balloon Fiesta* that was Sold Out and attended by 100,000 people. For this event, I obtained approval for our core marketing team to be in the press tent. On eclipse day, we gave away hundreds of eclipse glasses, eclipse books, and *MoonPies* to top media at dawn. These reporters had traveled from all over the U.S. to cover this event on the direct eclipse path. For this milestone event, I hired a second publicist (*Ann Flower PR*), and asked digital marketing professional Roberto Saenz (*Bazztiki Digital*) to be there to maximize results.

6. **Took Action Photos and Videos of the 2023 Annular Eclipse** —To gather authentic content for the client's visual assets library, our team gathered hundreds of creative photos and video on this eclipse trip. *APO's* marketing team was not available to attend, but I knew this event was a very important media opportunity. Fortunately, we watched this Ring of Fire eclipse with members of *NASA*. We all wore their custom eclipse glasses made by *APO*, which resulted in historic photos.

7. **Media Training** —To help the key media spokespeople look and sound great on-camera, *Goody PR* provided corporate executives, eclipse experts and authors with one-on-one media training. You can learn more in the Media Training Booster chapter.

8. **Created 26 Social Media Videos** —To support *APO's* digital marketing campaign, *Goody PR* also produced 26 *YouTube Shorts* and *Instagram Reels* at no extra charge. These short and creative clips were each under 1 minute. These multi-

purposed clips promoted *APO* products, which will be covered in the Digital Marketing Booster chapter.

Bonus Content: High Impact Tactic: Influencer Marketing

As a Bonus Content, consider Influencer Marketing as a PR Tactic. This approach has become a more essential part of marketing campaigns today because people trust authentic posts more than any paid ad.

For the *APO* campaign, our team asked influencers at the *ABQ International Balloon Fiesta* if we could take their photos wearing *APO*'s eclipse glasses. Most of them said yes, and their photos were used in TV coverage during Phase 2 of this publicity campaign. However, it was never a formal Influencer Marketing Campaign.

Your challenge is doing Influencer Marketing the right way. Without monitoring the content quality, this approach can backfire and hurt your reputation. To do it right, dive-in, be ready to invest, and embrace these tips.

If you are serious about doing Influencer Marketing, let's take a closer look at the HOW.

Top 10 Influencer Marketing Planning Tips

As a potential high-impact publicity tactic, consider using Influencer Marketing as part of a larger more comprehensive Public Relations Program. There are many options to consider, and you will need a budget to do it effectively.

Based on our research, here are our Top 10 Influencer Marketing Planning Tips:

1. Define your big-picture goals and timeline for your Influencer Marketing Campaign.

2. Define what are you promoting?

3. Create personality profiles for influencers who match your brand's ideal target audience. Research how to find influencers in your niche subject area. And then define

your ideal customer's age range, income level, hobbies and personality types.

4. Consider hiring Influencers to post unique and creative content about your brand for the biggest impact.

5. Determine your research approach. Will you be using software management tools to find influencers, and/or manually research and manage influencers?

6. Define clear content deliverables for influencers. For example, do you want influencers to post videos, photos and/or stories about your brand?

7. Research top influencers for your project, which may be in these groups:

   - Nano Influencers (1 – 10k Followers)
   - Micro-Influencers (10k – 100k Followers)
   - Mid-Tier Influencers (100k – 500k Followers)
   - Marco Influencers (500k – 1 Million Followers) and
   - Mega Influencers (1Million+ Followers)

8. Determine your Influencer Marketing Budget. Your costs may include:

   - Staffing/ Resources Costs.
   - Event Costs.
   - Software Tool Costs: *Influencer Hero, Afluencer, FeedSpot* and more.
   - Influencer Costs (You can try Affiliate Marketing where they get a commission if someone buys from a custom link. You can also pay for custom content. As an example, a Nano Influencer may charge $10/post while a Mega Influencer may charge $10,000/post on Instagram.)
   - Publicity Costs for promoting your initiative.

9. Write detailed contracts for Influencers with your deliverables clearly defined. Our PR colleague Susan Bejeckian specializes in travel PR. She finds the best influencers to visit her client destinations, reaches out online, and then writes a detailed contract. The influencer's travel costs are usually covered, and the contract outlines specific deliverables and content

ownership. In many cases, the influencer is asked to post a short series of video Reels. The process requires extensive research, planning and follow-up.

10. Lastly, track and measure your Influencer Marketing Results. You may want to create unique tracking codes and/or links to help you quantify the outcomes.

Influencer Marketing Example: *Bill Nye The Science Guy* and APO

As an influencer marketing example, *American Paper Optics* teamed up with *Bill Nye The Science Guy* and *The Planetary Society to* create a limited edition of commemorative eclipse glasses for the 2017 and 2024 Total Solar Eclipses.

This science celebrity is an American educator, actor, comedian, and engineer, who is best known for hosting the *PBS* children's show *Bill Nye the Science Guy. For the 2024 Total Solar Eclipse, Nye* hosted a watch party in Fredericksburg, Texas (north of San Antonio), and was actively promoting these custom eclipse glasses.

This partnership was a high impact tactic because @BillNye is well-known and has **3.6 million followers on *Instagram* alone**. Leading up to April 8th, Bill was all over the news educating people on eclipses and the importance of wearing eclipse glasses.

* * *

Your next step in developing a Creative Campaign is to build a content calendar.

2.3 Develop Your PR Program Campaign Calendar

In addition to developing your goals, objectives, budget, strategies and tactics, you want to create a Public Relations Program Campaign Calendar. This calendar should identify key dates and milestones. You can search online for national calendars with key dates and their meaning. For example, we often use the *National Day Calendar* or *National Today* website to identify relevant dates for our clients.

While there seems to be a day or even a month for everything now, it is very helpful to identify dates that can be included in a media pitch to make your subject more timely.

Without key dates or connections to headline news, your story is considered an "evergreen story." In this case, it can stay relevant for a long time, but is not urgent.

With so much breaking news, it's even harder to get coverage today. Use specific dates and months to draw attention faster to your company, product and/or book.

For the *APO* campaign, I did extensive research on dates connected to the two eclipses and science. These dates were often used in media pitches, along with digital marketing posts. The PR Strategy sent to the *APO* team included eclipse milestone dates.

You can set up your PR Campaign Calendar in Excel or use a shared drive on *Google Docs*, *SharePoint*, or other platforms, so everyone involved is in sync.

For our clients, *Goody PR* regularly drafts a calendar and reviews these dates as potential campaign themes and media hooks during PR meetings.

PR Calendar Date Examples

To give you some ideas for what can go on your PR Campaign Calendar, here are examples of themes and days that have attracted media for our clients:

Calendar Example 1: *Common Wisdom* **Author Dr. Laura Gabayan**

August: National Wellness Month

September: Self-Improvement Month

November: National Gratitude Month

March 26: National Science Appreciation Day

Event: *Barnes and Noble* LIVE Book Talk

Calendar Example 2: *Warriors Heart*: Addiction, PTSD and Mental Health Topics

January: National Depression Education and Awareness Month

February: National Dog Training Education Month

April: National Alcohol Awareness Month

Sept 10: World Suicide Prevention Day

Event: *Warriors Heart* Gallery public art display

Calendar Example 3: *Goody PR's Goody Business Book Awards* for Authors

March: National Reading Month

April 23: World Book Day

September: Read a New Book Month

November: National Entrepreneurship Month

Event: Annual Book Awards Announcement

Regularly Review Your Content Calendar

To ensure your PR success, continually review your PR calendars. You also want to periodically adjust your overall strategy, campaign themes and topics to get the best media results.

Case Study: National Dog Training Month Media Results

As an example of connecting a pitch to a national day or month, *Goody PR* is beyond grateful to have secured multiple stories for *Warriors Heart* during February's *National Dog Training Education Month* over several years. Their K-9 program for military, veterans and first responder clients is unique, and almost everyone LOVES dogs.

As a Superstar Media Spokesperson, *Warriors Heart's* K-9 Manager Michelle "Cash" Axmaker did several TV, print, radio and podcast interviews about how their program works as an Optional Elective for clients.

During these interviews, Cash explained how *Warriors Heart* trains Service Dogs and Emotional Support Dogs approximately 120 hours for each support behavior. As an example, a Service Dog may be trained to wake up a veteran up who is having a nightmare. And Cash is a Former Zookeeper, making her story unique.

This story magic resulted in many interviews every February.

***Warrior's Heart* K-9 Program Media Campaign Examples:**

In The Loop: AM 630 The Word & 930 AM the Answer **(Feb 2025)**
Cash Axmaker, *Warriors Heart*

***KENS5 CBS News San Antonio* (Feb 2024)**
At Bandera treatment facility, shelter dogs train to be emotional support and service dogs for military, veterans and law enforcement

***National Defense Radio Show* (Feb 2023)**
Warrior's Heart K9 Manager Michelle Axmaker

***KSAT ABC News San Antonio* (Feb 2022)**
How *Warriors Heart* K9 Program trains Service Dogs 120 Hours for One Support Behavior

* * *

There is a lot more involved in getting earned media coverage that will be discussed in this book. For now, use these Creative Campaign Booster Action Items as a foundation:

STEP 2: Your Creative Campaign Booster Action Items Recap

As you wrap up Step 2, use these 3 Creative Campaign Booster Action Items to boost your brand and media results.

2.1 Define Your Campaign Goals, Objectives and Budget

Work with your client to clearly define your campaign's big picture goals, theme, target market, and budget. Document these elements at the beginning of every campaign.

2.2 Identify Strategies and Tactics

Once you have your overall objectives, start working on a detailed strategy document with the Who, What and How for implementing your innovative creative campaign. And as a bonus step, include Influencer Marketing as a high impact tactic.

2.3 Develop Your PR Campaign Calendar

After you've defined the big picture publicity strategy and tactics, start researching your key calendar months and days. Put everything together on a shared Public Relations Program calendar so everyone is in sync.

So start singing *Come and Get Your Love Now* as you prepare to launch your Public Relations Program and Publicity Campaign. You're now you're get ready to start your Media Outreach.

PART 2

GAIN POSITIVE PRESS VALUE

Get free publicity and increase your credibility and sales using our 3Ms: Media Outreach, Media Training and Media Relations Boosters.

MEDIA OUTREACH BOOSTER:
Develop Unique Story Hooks to Secure Top Media

I'm hooked on a feeling.
I'm high on believing.
That you're in love with me.

–*Hooked On A Feeling* by Blue Swede

What makes media outreach like dating is that you must find the right reporter at the right time who falls in love with your story. You want to find a journalist who believes so much in your unique story and mission that they are genuinely excited to share it with the world —for free.

As background, there are many different types of media you can contact. Who you reach out to often depends on the outlet and their job title. For example, you may want to pitch a news producer, assignment desk manager, anchor, multimedia journalist, freelance producer, editor, columnist, freelance writer, radio show host, and/ or podcast host.

Most reporters are looking for new material to make you —and them —look great to their audience. And the best way to break through all of the noise is to write a powerful media hook that is timely, relevant and emotionally connects on multiple levels.

Throughout this book, you've already been reading great media examples to give you insights on what works versus what makes a reporter pass. This chapter will help you advance by describing how to find and pitch reporters. You will find more insider secrets, case studies and reporter insights.

So let's take a closer look at these 3 Media Outreach Boosters.

STEP 3: Media Outreach Boosters

3.1 Research Top Media who will Love Your Story

3.2 Pitch Powerful Media Hooks with a Unique Story

3.3 Prepare Your Press Kits and Story Visuals

If you're running a small business, investing in ongoing public relations can be more effective than paid ads. To increase your chances of getting coverage, you must reach out to the right reporters versus any reporter.

For the 2024 Total Solar Eclipse, the topic was trending, yet there were many companies competing for the limited TV and radio air time, along with print/digital space. Similarly, your challenge is to develop a compelling media hook that results in a story.

And if your pitch is not urgent, re-think the approach to make it more timely.

So let's get started with the best practices for Media Outreach.

3.1 Research Top Media who will Love Your Story

Your best overall strategy for Media Outreach is to start at the 30,000 foot level and identify who really cares about your industry or expertise. Then research to find the best reporters in your niche subject area(s).

This media research process can take hours to get the best results, so don't try to fast-track your approach.

Because Media Outreach can be so challenging, many people hire a marketing and/or PR agency to help them stand out. Yes, it's an investment. But keep in mind that the professionals have the tools, experience and contacts to fast-track this process for you.

If you are ready to do a lot of heavy lifting and be resilient, this chapter can provide you with the steps needed to reach out to the media and secure interviews.

Based on our experience, you are the salesperson to the media for either your brand and/or your client. Every story usually takes 2-20 follow-ups with the reporter to actually get an interview request, schedule a meeting, and then follow-up to get it published.

The key to your success is how you make the reporter FEEL, which is why I chose the song *Hooked on a Feeling* for this chapter. If the reporter is not moved, inspired, or having an aha moment after reading your pitch, it's going to be very hard to get coverage.

You can reach out to reporters via email (usually the best way), phone (it's really hard to get someone to answer, but it's worth trying), and/or text. ONLY text a reporter if they gave you their cell, and you have a media relationship with them. And even if they know you well, text sparingly.

So let's discuss how you find journalists to cover your story.

Research Earned Media Types and Wish List Outlets

You always want to research media outlets and reporters based on their media type, which includes TV, print/digital, and radio/podcasts. Make a Media Wish List with your preferred outlets in an Excel spreadsheet, and then start researching their contact information.

1. **Find TV Reporters** —To secure TV interviews on top media such as the *TODAY Show, CNN* and/or any local TV station, it's not easy to find the best contact. In many cases, a specific TV reporter or producer will hide their email. You can pay thousands of dollars to access media databases such as *Cision*, and their contact information may still be hidden. Honestly, reporters often get bombarded with hundreds, if not thousands, of pitches every day, so of course they guard their contact information.

    In general, the bigger the outlet, the harder it will be to find media contact information.

    So you must get creative. You may be able to guess their email format, call a local TV newsroom, check their personal website or social media and/or research via *Google* search or AI to find ways to reach them.

2. **Find Print/Digital Journalists** —To secure print or digital interviews for publications such as *Fast Company, Forbes* or *WebMD*, you can use any of the methods above. Sometimes a list of reporters is on the publication's masthead.

    In addition, you can message a reporter via social media. I have used this approach on *LinkedIn* and *Instagram* with some success. However, you need to walk softly when reaching out through these channels. Your best bet is to get to know them first, and then send a personalized message.

Instead of sending a long email on *LinkedIn*, ask if it is ok to send to them a pitch —and then ask for their best email.

3. **Find Radio and Podcast Hosts** —With approximately 4.6 million+ podcasts in 2026, you can get really lost searching for the right podcast Host or Producer to pitch. I highly recommend that you search for only the top podcasts in your subject area. You can use different podcast matching tools such as *PodSeeker, PodMatch, PodPitch, Matchmaker. fm, and Talks.co.*

    Your challenge is researching the show's audience data to determine if you even want to be a guest. Search for their average monthly reach, average number of downloads per show, engagement rates, and demographics. Keep in mind that accurate podcast numbers are almost impossible to find, and often don't match up.

Let's take a closer look at a confusing podcast data example:

Bonus Content: Podcast Data Research Example

As part of your podcast research process, ListenNotes.com will tell you if it is a Top Podcast (1percent, 5 percent, 10 percent) based on their formula. While nothing is foolproof with podcast data, *Listen Notes* is based on the show's Listen Score (0-100) and Global Rank. They also use a mathematical model that combines different data sources to score each show. If there is no ranking, then you know it's not a top podcast.

Podcast Research Example: Data Doesn't Add Up

As a podcast data example, *Goody PR* received an interview request for a client from "XYZ Podcast" (this really happened, but their name is not provided). The host wanted to charge my client a fee for the interview, and boasted about huge numbers that did not match our research.

When I searched on other paid podcast research tools, it said the average number of downloads was much lower than what the host promised.

XYZ Podcast Numbers from Host

- Unique Monthly Visits: On Average = 141,374
- Daily average listeners (estimated) = 4,116

XYZ Podcast Numbers on paid Podcast Research Tool

- Monthly Listeners = 2,600
- Listeners per episode = 45

Because our clients don't pay for media 99 percent of the time, I explained that it was a pass to the host. Fortunately, I was able to negotiate the interview for free, and the client was happy to proceed.

The way podcasts should work is that the guest is providing great content for free to entertain and educate their listeners. The host then finds show sponsors to cover their production costs. If a host wants to charge you to be their guest on their podcast, it is a lazy way out IMHO.

* * *

You should also research podcast social media followers, number of reviews, average ranking for reviews, and read the positive/ negative comments.

And don't forget to listen to the show to see if the Host's style and format are a match for your brand. If the host is a solid expert, asks guests great questions, and speaks to your target audience, consider doing an interview, even if it's not a top podcast.

For example, one of our former clients sold real estate investments in another country. Their main goal was to reach their niche audience by being a guest on real estate investing podcasts. This focused approach worked well for her business because it reached her target audience faster. If only ten people listened, and she got a lead or sale, it was well worth the time and investment in a podcast publicity campaign.

Find the Right Reporters in Your Niche Subject Areas

Once you've thought about the types of media and outlets that you want to prioritize, your next step is to research where your target market gets their news. Are they watching cable news, local news; reading magazines, newspapers, blogs, *Substack*: and/or listening to podcasts?

Then research how to contact specific reporters who are mostly likely to be interested.

To find the right reporters for your niche subject area, read the reporter's bio and recent stories to see if there are any connectors. For example, if you are a wellness expert with a diet book, find a reporter who writes for *Everyday Health* about nutrition.

Keep in mind that there are thousands of reporters at top media outlets such as *CNN, The Wall Street Journal* or *NPR*. Your challenge is to go on a treasure hunt to find the best reporter.

5 Media Research Examples by Subject Area:

To give you more Media Outreach ideas, let's look closer at 5 research examples based on different subject areas that *Goody PR* specializes in for clients:

Media Research Example 1 — Small Business Product Reporters

For our eclipse glasses publicity campaign, *Goody PR* primarily pitched Meteorologists, Scientists and Newsrooms across the United States about how the eclipse glasses were made and tested to protect your eyes while viewing the Total Solar Eclipse.

Almost everyone was covering this trending story, and we were grateful to get coverage on the *TODAY Show, CBS Saturday Morning, NewsNation, Scripps News, People Magazine, USA Today, NPR, podcasts and many local TV.*

I also identified reporters more likely to cover eclipse glasses, who were located on the two eclipse paths where there was more buzz. The direct eclipse path for the Total Solar Eclipse included 15 U.S. states. As a result, I researched news outlets in cities there. Using this strategy, you can see where stories were secured on the direct eclipse paths below.

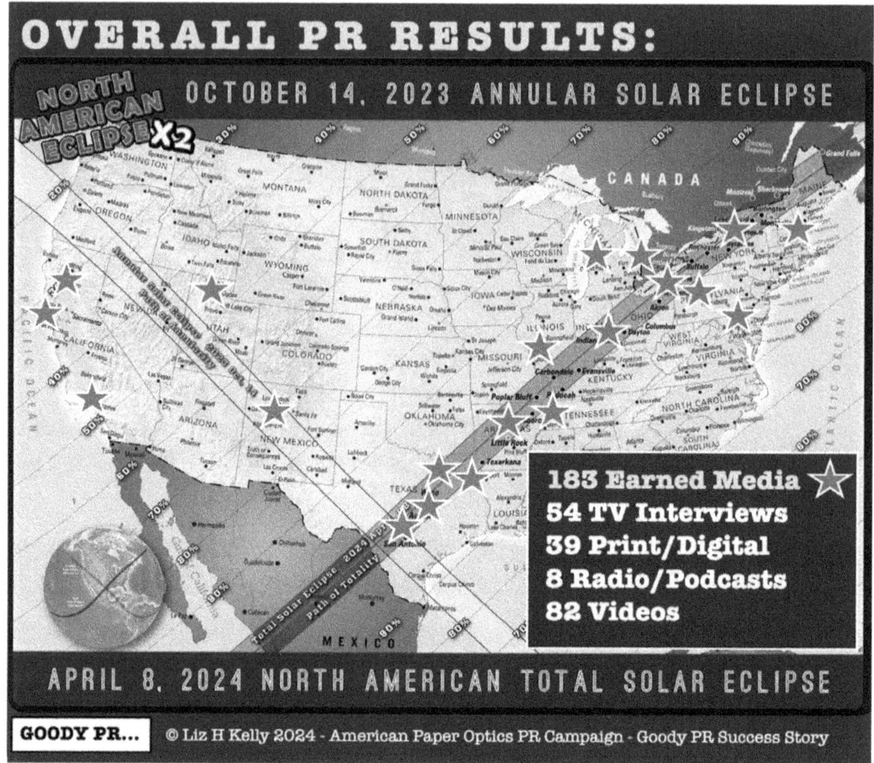

Media Research Example 2 — Health and Wellness Reporters

If you are looking to reach health and wellness reporters for your business or book, research journalists who specialize in your topic. Depending on your expertise, *Psychology Today*, *SheKnows* and *WebMD* could be great media matches.

You can also ask newspaper and magazine reporters what topics are on their editorial calendar since print outlets plans months in advance. While you may not get a reply, it helps if you know them.

In one case, a reporter from *Woman's World* magazine featured our client in a story about how to manage stress over the holidays. When I thanked her profusely, I also asked about her 2026 editorial calendar. She replied, "I've recently stepped away from our emotional wellness beat and am taking on more 'hard health' topics from heart disease to diabetes to menopause. If you have any doctors or nutritionists in your stable, please let me know! Looking forward to working with you again soon!"

Reporters are all very different, and they are not always looking for stories. To provide you with more insights, I interviewed a freelance writer and podcast host about his process for selecting stories and guests.

Bonus Content: Reporter Insights from Christopher Littrell
Police1 Freelance Writer and *Gravity Podcast* Host

As a Freelancer Writer and Podcast Host, Christopher Littrell shared honest feedback with me to help you with your media outreach.

Freelance Writers and Podcast Hosts work very differently than many journalists in traditional media. Most of these freelancers get paid very little and work LONG HOURS to cover your story — because you earned their respect. Freelancers often feel a higher calling to tell stories that support their purpose in life.

Christopher's personal background impacts the stories he decides to cover. As a retired Law Enforcement Officer (25 years), *U.S. Air Force* Veteran, *Gravity Podcast* Host, Leadership and Wellness Consultant, Workplace Safety Expert, Speaker/Trainer and Author, *Echoes from the Street: A Police Officer's Journey Through Trauma, Recovery, and Redemption* (2026), he primarily covers first responder insights, including mental health and recovery stories as a Freelancer for *Police1*.

Media Outreach Advice Tips

When asked for advice tips, Christopher shared; *there are probably a lot of things going on in the lives of freelancers and podcast hosts, so you can't assume anything.*

You need to research the reporter or host's background and purpose and find connectors.

A Freelance Reporter's Process

Christopher expanded on his process:

Most of my writings begin when I have an idea, and I pitch the story to the editor. I write the title with a summary, and then the editor says Yes or No.

Sometimes an editor gets back to me, and sometimes I never hear back. A no response is a No, and they owe me nothing. So if someone does not reply, I don't consider it rude.

Then, of course, there is an exception to every rule. If my editor reaches out to me and says, what about this story, but that's not my normal process, I am always open to their ideas.

And even if the article is pre-approved by an editor, sometimes the written story doesn't get published.

How *Gravity Podcast* Host selects Guests

For his *Gravity Podcast*, Christopher explained:

I get at least 1-2 inquiries a week from people saying, can I be on your podcast —or they are representing a variety of people whom they want to discuss —and I don't reply to any of them because I already have 50+ people whom I want to interview.

In many cases, a Podcast Host is reaching out to the guests they want, so you really have to stand out and explain why your overall message is in alignment with their show.

In this case, Littrell added, For Podcast Guests, I've sent interview requests to U.S. Presidents and celebrities —and some people have actually told me YES and were on the podcast —but I don't have any expectations.

ABOUT: Christopher Littrell is a Christian, husband, father, *USAF* veteran, retired police officer, endurance athlete, and storyteller committed to helping others experience life change. For more information, visit ChristopherLittrell.com

Media Research Example 3 —Business Leader Reporters

If you are a CEO and/or Leadership Coach, your best bet is to find a business editor or reporter who writes profiles of thought leaders and/or entrepreneurs. To be truly successful, find a business reporter who is more interested in writing about your company's growth, milestones and/or a new product launch.

For example, think about sharing unique insights about something you created, your company's backstory, and/or a study that makes you stand out. Great publications for you may include *Entrepreneur, Fast Company, The Business Journals* and/or *Forbes.*

Media Outreach Example: *Fast Company* Story in Niche Unique Business Thought Leader and Author Insights

As an example of a niche business reporter, I was fortunate to find a *Fast Company* reporter who specializes in productivity, careers and leadership. Their column was in alignment with our business thought leader client. Based on his backstory as a General Manager, helpful tips and leadership books, she covered his practice.

The unique pitch that got a YES resulted in this headline:

Don't hire someone because of their resume. Look for this instead.

Unique Story Topic: Omar L. Harris shared why it's important to hire based on behavior instead of a resume. He developed this unique hiring process and mindset that the author describes in his book, *Be a J.E.D.I Leader, Not a Boss.*

Thought Leader Backstory: As an organizational leadership cons-ultant/founder, Omar was a former GM at major health organi-zations. While working for *GlaxoSmithKline* (GSK) and *Allergan* pharmaceuticals, he managed 800+ people and developed this unique hiring process.

Media Research Example 4 —Finance and Wealth Management Reporters

If your business is focused on helping people save money on taxes and/or protecting their personal or business assets, your target audience is going to be very different.

Search online for the best reporters who cover your topic, and pitch a unique subject that they have not covered in the past (easier said than done). Some of the best media outlets who've done positive press for our clients related to wealth management include *GOBankingRates, MSN, CNBC, and FOX Business.*

Media Research Example 5 - Entertainment Reporters

If you are an Executive Producer, Director and/or Actor in the entertainment industry with a new project (TV show, movie, web series, or book), you want to reach out to a very different group of reporters for potential coverage.

For this niche, it's easier to get film coverage if your movie is shown at film festivals. Fortunately, I covered movies at film festivals for 11+ years at the *Sundance Film Festival, TCM, Comic-Con* and more for *The Huffington Post, Examiner, Red Carpet Report and Pasadena Weekly*. It helped me better understand first-hand what it's like to do red carpet interviews and coverage.

As a publicist, I've done entertainment PR for Executive Producer Garrett Z. Sutton and Emmy Award ® Winning Director Greg DeHart for their two documentary film projects, *Symphony of the Holocaust* and *Max Patkin: The Clown Prince of Baseball*. Because these films had a higher purpose and message, they got more coverage.

Their award-winning film, *Symphony of the Holocaust*, was featured on *FOX 11 Los Angeles, Spectrum News Ohio, NPR WOSU Public Radio, The Las Vegas Review Journal cover story, CBS Las Vegas, 2 News Nevada*, and many others. When this film was submitted for Oscar consideration for Best Documentary Feature, this update was in the trade magazines: *Variety, The Hollywood Reporter, Deadline, and The Wrap*.

It's always the backstory behind a film or book that gets you media coverage.

And if you are a celebrity, you will get a lot more entertainment media coverage because they want the star power. For a PR campaign, *Modern Family's* Executive Producer and *Emmy®* Award Winner Danny Zuker hired us to promote a timely book that had nothing to do with his show. However, because of his celebrity status, *TMZ, TheWrap, The Hollywood Reporter, CNN, FOX 11 Los Angeles, KTLA, Dr. Drew KABC Radio, Howard Stern*, and many other outlets covered his book.

Your media outreach challenge is that entertainment is a very popular niche, so the more specific you are in searching for the best reporter, the better.

3.2 Pitch Powerful Media Hooks with a Unique Story

A media hook is a potential headline with a powerful story that moves both the reporter and their audience. It's an attention grabber that gets a reporter to look at your pitch. It's the teaser that the reporter says, "Coming up next, we will cover…" that gets you to keep watching that channel.

To get reporters to stop and pay attention to your pitch, your media hook should highlight your Wow Story that you learned how to write in Step 1: Story Magic Booster.

Showcase your media hook in your email subject line, opening line of a pitch, and/or in the potential story headline. Put it at the top of your email in a bigger font that is bold.

You also want to be honest with yourself. If you reach out to reporters, and there is no interest, it's probably time to revise your media hook. You can always send follow-up pitches with edited headlines, but be prepared to change your approach completely if no one is asking for interviews.

Let's look at examples of catchy email subject lines, media outreach timing tips from reporters and then our ten unique media hook examples for the Award-Winning *APO/* Eclipse Glasses Campaign.

Pitch with a Catchy Email Subject Line

When reaching out to reporters, the most important part of your pitch is the email subject line. If you don't grab their attention immediately, the reporter, host or producer probably won't even open your email.

To pique their interest, write a catchy email subject line with your media hook. For our media outreach, I usually write the word PITCH or MEDIA ALERT in the subject line.

You should use PITCH if you want them to cover a feature story that is not urgent. If your media hook is related to an event or day, you can also add the word "Timely" to your email subject line.

Use MEDIA ALERT if you are sending a news story that is connected to an announcement, launch and/or event. Your story is urgent, and is often connected to headline news.

Your best approach for media outreach is to email an individual reporter with a personal note. While you can also call, most reporters prefer email pitches. For example, you might compliment them for another story they wrote.

Another great way to get a story covered is to offer an EXCLUSIVE. In this case, you usually want to provide a deadline so that you can offer the story to other reporters if they pass.

You can also send an email blast to a customized list of reporters who cover a specific subject area related to you or your client's niche. To effectively send an email blast, always do extensive research on the reporters' job titles, subject areas and recent stories. If a reporter has not written a story in three years, there is probably no need to pitch them.

You can use email marketing tools to personalize the subject line with the outlet name. Within the email body, address the reporter by first name and mention their outlet.

It's important to note that you must legally have an Opt-Out for your email blasts. If you use a tool like *Constant Contact, Mailchimp or Hubspot*, these features are provided and manage this process for you. Otherwise, you need to manually manage requests.

To help you better understand what works best, here are five subject lines that resulted in national publicity for our clients:

5 Subject Line Examples resulting in National Media Coverage

MEDIA ALERT for *NewsNation* —Timely —How to Easily Identify Real versus Fake Eclipse Glasses

PITCH for *CNN This Morning* —Timely —Unique Marine Veteran and *Warriors Heart* COO Recovery Story

MEDIA ALERT for *American City Business Journals* —Timely for Small Business with New Overtime Pay Announcement in May

Timely Pitch for *Fast Company* —Great Rehiring Surge Solution — Hiring based on Behaviors vs. Resume

PITCH for *What's Health Got to Do with It?* —Timely —Doctor — How to be a Champion of Your Health for 2026 (*NPR* affiliate)

* ● *

These subject lines are shared to give you creative ideas for how to get a reporter to actually open your email pitch. You can also test different email subject lines to different groups, and see what gets a higher open rate. This process can take time to fine-tune.

In addition to writing a catchy subject line, you must find the best time to contact reporters.

Timing is Everything for TV Reporters

To increase your chances of a response, you always want to consider the best time to reach out to a reporter. And this timing will vary depending on many factors.

You want to think about the reporter's schedule, and find the best days and times to pitch. Usually, sending out email pitches or calling on Tuesday –Thursday mornings is best. However, I saw an incredible response to an email pitch sent on a Sunday afternoon. It was related to an event on Tuesday and resulted in three TV interview requests for Monday.

For TV reporters, always avoid contacting them during a live news broadcast when they are super busy and focused.

Bonus Content: *ABC News* TV Reporter Insights

To help you decide the best times to pitch a TV reporter, I interviewed former *KSAT ABC News* Reporter Jonathan Cotto to get his honest feedback.

Fortunately, I worked with Jonathan for three years on multiple stories for three clients. It was a solid media relationship, which is exactly what you want to build. When he left *KSAT ABC News* for a new Communications job, I congratulated him. And then, I kept in touch for many reasons.

When I asked Jonathan for insights on media outreach, he emphasized that for TV, you must research which newscast a reporter is assigned to. For example, a reporter assigned to the 6PM, 10PM, or 7AM news have very different schedules. He recommends approaching them during times that don't conflict with their shows.

Jonathan added, "Once you approach a TV Producer or Assignment Manager, make sure that you've done your homework the night before or early morning. See what is trending. See what story can turn around the same day."

This TV reporter feedback is invaluable. It also confirms why you must always be reading the news for TV pitches and know what is trending. Every morning I spend at least thirty minutes reading the headlines on different news apps. Add this action item to your list.

Let's now take a closer look at how to define a unique media hook.

Media Hook Example:

How Revised Pitch resulted in National TV Interviews

A pitch is always based on a media hook with a unique story. This process is an art that requires a lot of critical thinking. You want to have an open mind, ask a lot of questions and seek a deeper understanding of potential topics to find the media gold. And remember, it's never about your great company or new book.

For the *APO* / Eclipse Glasses national publicity campaign, the client really wanted to focus pitches on eye safety tips for watching eclipses. While that topic was important, every Meteorologist and *NASA* Scientist was already talking about that topic – with authority.

To fine-tune this media hook, I changed the angle a little to make the client stand out. Our revised media hook was more unique and told their story better. The stronger potential headline was: **How Eclipse Glasses are Made and Tested for Your Eye Safety by the biggest U.S. manufacturer.**

This revised Media Hook idea came to us like a lightning bolt on our daily walks. There were few experts actually making eclipse glasses. This new approach made a significant difference and resulted in more national publicity coverage.

I also got b-roll footage of the factory from the CMO to add context. These short video clips were shown in many national TV interviews as a behind-the-scenes visual.

* * *

To get record-breaking results for our *APO/* Eclipse Glasses campaign, the team came up with ten unique stories with multiple spokespeople. You cannot rely on one media hook alone.

10 Unique Media Hooks for National Publicity Campaign

For our Award-Winning Public Relations Program and Publicity Campaign, I worked closely with *APO's* CMO and the digital marketing team to identify ten unique media hooks. This creative campaign process is how we were able to achieve 183 unique earned media stories (TV, print, radio, podcasts and video) for free in only 8.5 months. This type of result is off-the-charts for a product.

As a result of the combination of these ten different media hooks and many other factors, this campaign went viral.

1. **How Eclipse Glasses are Made and Tested for Your Eye Safety** —This unique media hook was the top pitch and a gamechanger that secured national coverage.

2. **How to Safely View an Eclipse** —This hot topic had more competition from other experts. Our favorite story included *APO's* CEO with an eye doctor on *KSL NBC News* in Salt Lake City, Utah. After I sent out this pitch, the producer came up with the idea to include two complementary experts.

3. **Real vs. Fake Eclipse Glasses** —To help people worried about fake eclipse glasses that could cause blindness, *APO* was on top of this issue and showed examples. The CMO also created an infographic with "The Core 4" verification process to educate consumers on how to tell if eclipse glasses are real. This infographic was shown in several TV interviews as a great visual.

4. *Solar Snap: The Eclipse App and Kit* —To help consumers take great eclipse photos with their smartphone, Astronomer and Hubble Space Telescope team member Dr. Doug Duncan invented *Solar Snap: The Eclipse App and Kit.* Doug worked with *APO* to produce and sell this kit with filters to protect your phone. You also had to download the *Solar Snap Eclipse App.* This topic was very popular!

5. **Children's Eclipse Book: *The Moonies: Journey to the Total Solar Eclipse*** - Author Meg Jerit wrote a unique children's story based on her personal backstory. This illustrated book included alien characters who travel from Mars to Austin, Texas, for the Total Solar Eclipse. They run into some issues on their way, and the book is loosely based on Meg's real-life experience watching the 2017 Total Solar Eclipse.

6. **Small Business Administrator Factory Visit** —As a small business success story, *APO*'s factory was visited by the *U.S. Small Business Association.* In this case, *APO* was asked NOT to tell anyone, and background checks were done. Then suddenly, they asked me to notify the media the day before at 4PM about a press conference the next morning at 9AM. It was a scramble to send out Media Alerts and secure coverage. Fortunately, every local TV station and *The Memphis Business Journal* covered it.

7. **Eclipse Glasses for a Cause** —This social good campaign supported *APO*'s goal to give back to the community through two custom eclipse glasses to benefit *St. Jude Children's Research Hospital* and *The ALS Association.* Both stories were personally connected to Paulo Aur, CFO/COO and co-owner, which made it even more moving.

8. **Eclipse Education Support for Schools and Libraries —** To help educate students about eclipses, *APO* sent a gift package to a science teacher and librarian at a school in Boston. *NBC10 Boston* covered their science class where the teacher taught them about eclipse glasses and safety tips. In addition, *APO* made millions of custom eclipse glasses for the national *SEAL Program (Solar Eclipse Activities for Libraries)* funded by the *Gordon and Betty Moore Foundation.*

9. **Eclipse Weekend Wedding —**This unique wedding story was discussed in our first chapter about Story Magic Boosters. The couple's custom diamond ring effect eclipse glasses and backstory were covered by *KENS5 CBS News* San Antonio.

10. **Top 10 Collectibles and Celebrations —**Our last media hook was designed to reach travel reporters. It highlighted custom eclipse glasses for different events across the U.S. For example, Cleveland's *Rock and Roll Hall of Fame* hosted a *SolarFest* with cool eclipse glasses made by *APO*.

3.3 Prepare Press Materials with 5 Key Elements

Your final step in this Media Outreach process is to prepare your press materials, which includes your pitch, press kits and story visuals. Once you've created your media lists, you want to have these materials ready to send reporters. When you get an interview request, things can happen very fast —so you want to be ready.

Many outlets, especially TV, are going to ask you for potential visuals. For print, radio and podcast interviews, they are more likely to ask for a headshot photo and short bio.

When you are watching TV, those images do not just magically appear. A publicist or guest sent the producer the images to add value to their story. Each media outlet has a graphics team managing the production behind-the-scenes that you will never see.

Your job is to make it Really Easy for Reporters to tell your story!

You want to create a clear, concise and compelling pitch and have a digital press kit ready to send. Include key information about the media spokesperson and insights.

5 Must Haves for Pitches and Press Kits

1. Expert's Name and Title —Keep it short so that it fits on a TV banner.

2. Expert's Short Bio —Send one paragraph only.

3. Potential Visuals —Put your photos and videos on a shared *Google Drive*.

4. Potential Q and A — Send potential interview questions and answers.

5. Main Website Address — Provide one URL only to avoid confusion.

So let's take a closer look at each of these five items with a case study example.

1. Expert's Name and Title — Keep it short so it fits on a TV banner

For *Corporate Direct* CEO/Founder, Award-Winning Author, and Asset Protection Attorney Garrett Sutton, here is what I've sent in pitches with his title and short bio.

Short Title Example for TV:

Garrett Sutton, CEO/Founder *Corporate Direct* and Author

2. Expert's Short Bio — Send one paragraph only

Your short bio should highlight your credibility as a trusted thought leader. It should tell the reporter why you are a great source, your personal WHY, media experience, and a few fun facts as connectors. You want the reporter to feel confident about choosing YOU as the spokesperson.

While this media interview means the world to you and your brand, your media contact's reputation is also on the line. A producer wants to select people who can clearly tell a story in a non-promotional way with insider tips, insights and inspiration.

Your short bio can help a producer make a quick decision about whether to book you.

Short Bio Examples

Really Short Bio:

Garrett Sutton is the CEO/Founder *Corporate Direct*, Asset Protection Attorney, Rich Dad Advisor to Robert Kiyosaki (Author, *Rich Dad Poor Dad*), *TENERO* Financial Education *YouTube* Channel Host, and Bestselling Author of 11 financial education books, who has transformed legal protection primarily for entrepreneurs, real estate investors and digital asset investors.

Better Bio for Pitches:

ABOUT: GARRETT SUTTON (Reno, Nevada) is the *Corporate Direct* Founder/CEO, *Sutton Law* Founder, Award-Winning Author of 11 books, Asset Protection Attorney, Rich Dad's 25-Year Legal Architect of Business Protection and trusted advisor to Robert Kiyosaki (*Rich Dad Poor Dad*). For 35+ years, Garrett Sutton's *Corporate Direct* has been transforming legal protection primarily for entrepreneurs, real estate investors and digital asset investors by forming and maintaining corporations and LLCs to protect their personal assets in all 50 states. His goal is to help entrepreneurs and investors maintain their privacy and advance their financial goals. Garrett's bestselling books have sold over 1 million copies worldwide, including *Start Your Own Corporation* and *Loopholes of Real Estate*. His work has appeared on *BBC World News —Talking Business, FOX and Friends, Newsmax, Spectrum News, CBS KTVN Reno, ABC News Reno*, and in *Forbes, MSN, GoBankingRates*, and many top podcasts. Outside of the office, Garrett likes to ski, go to baseball games, produce movies and write.

3. Potential Visuals —Put your photos and videos on a shared *Google Drive*

For potential visuals, make sure that you send high-quality images and video with good lighting to reporters. While these visual storytelling tips may sound obvious, everyone is not a photographer, despite the majority having a smartphone with a camera. If your photos are dark with shadows, edit them —or don't send them at all.

And if you are a publicist, it's your job to guide your client through this process. Quality check the visuals, and ask for more if needed. Trust me, your client and the reporter will thank you for asking for better visuals.

For your image file size, they should be at least 500KB as a JPEG, JPG, or PNG. A smaller size can significantly lower the quality of the story.

For your video, the format should be landscape versus vertical. The video quality should be at least 720p resolution with a display size of 1280 x 720 pixels.

You NEVER want to attach images to an email for security reasons, unless you are specifically asked to by the reporter. Instead, make it really easy for them to download your visuals by sending a recognizable *Google Drive* URL.

And to make it even easier for reporters, number and name each visual. As a result, they can quickly scan the files to determine what images and b-roll video to use.

Lastly, make sure you tell them who to credit for your visuals. In most cases, I give the client's website address.

4. Potential Q and A —Send potential interview questions and answers.

When you pitch story ideas to reporters and/or send a press kit, it's best to send 3-5 Potential Questions and Answers with insights from the media spokesperson.

For a Digital Press Kit, you can also create a Media One Sheet with frequently asked questions. Post this summary as a PDF in your *Google Drive*. You can also print a hard copy for press kit and book mailings.

The media is overwhelmed with detail, and does not have time to research everything about you, your business and/or book. Every client wants a reporter to read their entire book, watch their movie and/or know everything about their brand. The reality is that there is not enough time in the day for most reporters to do that level of research.

Of course, you are so proud of your work that you want to share everything about you, your company, book and/or product. However, it's best to get right to the point in all of your communications and interviews.

With the average attention span of an adult being 8 seconds, you must be clear, concise and compelling. This is the main message in my previous how-to book: *8-Second PR: New Public Relations Crash Course.*

Your Q and A answers should include a maximum of 1-2 short sentence answers. It should be written like soundbites that you might say on TV. While some publicists, say, just send the questions in a pitch, I prefer to send short-answer responses.

Bonus Content: National TV Producer Opinion on Pitch Format

To help you, I asked a top cable news network producer, whom I've been fortunate to work with several times, for her opinion on pitch formats. Below is our text exchange:

Liz, Publicity Question: *As a reporter, do you like pitches where the Q and A has the answers spelled out, or is it better just to send the questions with no answers? I get mixed feedback on this, so I would appreciate any thoughts.*

Jen, Producer Answer: *I like the pitches with the Q and A scripted out. I like to know what the person I'm interviewing is going to* *say. It often sparks new conversations if I know their point of view ahead of time.*

I can't emphasize enough the importance of making your pitches and press materials clear and concise to help journalists tell your story.

5. Main Website Address — Provide 1 URL Only to avoid confusion

Your ultimate publicity goal is to build awareness, credibility and sales for your business or product. To do this effectively, share only the main website address in interviews. While it's great if you wear multiple hats, keep-it-simple and focused with one URL.

I also do not recommend broadly saying, "You can find my book on *Amazon*." Every book should be on *Amazon* because it's the world's biggest bookseller. However, your title may not show up in the *Amazon* search results (more on this later).

And don't wait for a reporter to ask you, where can I find out more, because they may not. Your job is to share your website as part of a conversation. For example, you might say, "If you want to learn more tips or find helpful resources, go to XYZ.com."

After every interview, you want to get a text like this one from a reporter whom I was fortunate to work with on a morning show feature interview:

Media Relations Win!

"Thank you for being so thorough
and concise, it's so refreshing."

–Clarke, Great Day SA Co-Host, KENS5 CBS San Antonio

Your job is to manage your Media Outreach and Media Relations so they will want you to come back as a repeat guest.

Always remember that a reporter and/or producer are people with feelings and personal challenges, just like you. So walk softly, treat them with respect, thank them profusely, share their story on social media - and tag the outlet and reporter.

You are now ready to be fearless in your Media Outreach. So do your research, and get ready to pitch the right reporters at the right time.

STEP 3: Your Media Outreach Booster Action Items Recap

As you wrap up this chapter, here are your 3 Media Outreach Booster Action Items to boost your brand and media results.

3.1 Research Top Media who will Love Your Story

Do some heavy-lifting research to find the best media who are most likely to fall in love with your story and topic. This research is an on-going process, but you have to start, so draft 3 Media Lists based on job title, outlet, niche, and geography.

3.2 Pitch Powerful Media Hooks with a Unique Story

To develop an Award-Winning Publicity Campaign, create 5-10 unique media hooks that you can pitch reporters. Use these media hooks to write a catchy email subject line that grabs their attention. Make sure your topic emotionally connects with story magic to get the reporters to say Yes.

3.3 Prepare Press Materials with 5 Key Elements

Prepare press materials with five key elements for each media hook, pitch and spokesperson. In your pitch email and press kits, send 3-5 Questions and Answers. Get your digital press kit set up on a *Google Drive* to share high resolution photos and videos safely. And make it really clear whom to credit for your visuals.

And remember our PR mantra, "Be patient and persistent, and never desperate" with everyone you meet on your *award-winning publicity* journey.

MEDIA TRAINING BOOSTER:
Be a Superstar Media Spokesperson

> Don't stop believin'.
> Hold on to that feeling.

–Journey by Escape

Do you want to know the secrets for how to look and sound like a Superstar Media Spokesperson, who is recognized as an authentic, credible and trustworthy source? While it looks so easy on TV for many talking heads, the reality is that it takes time to master these communications skills. Most of these pundits have had hours of media training and interview experience so their message is impactful.

When I pitch potential guests to TV producers, the national outlets will often ask to see a video example of the spokesperson. Because their job is to find great guests, they want to see how you show up on camera and present key points.

To get you prepared to be a Superstar Media Spokesperson, let's take a closer look at the three Media Training Boosters in this chapter.

STEP 4: Media Training Boosters

4.1 Set Stage for Your Interview Success

4.2 Be a Great Visual with High-Quality Sound during Interviews

4.3 Use Storytelling and Soundbites to Connect Emotionally

These insider tips are based on my personal experience doing 30+ national and local TV interviews as an author, along with our *Goody PR* Media Training program for clients. To prepare our clients for primarily TV and radio interviews, I've done both one-on-one coaching and training classes in person and via *Zoom*. This step is beyond important, so take notes!

If you are a CEO, CMO or business owner, don't let your ego stop you from getting media training and doing practice sessions, especially before a major interview. It's a unique skill, and it's really important to get coaching from experts who have been there, done that —and can provide you with honest feedback.

Taking time out of your busy schedule for media training can increase your confidence, delivery, and potential business impacts. With the right guidance, practice and honest feedback, you are much more likely to boost both your personal and business brands.

4.1 Set Stage for Your Interview Success

Just like preparing to launch a business, book or even a rocket launch, you always want to follow preparation steps to ensure success. Remember, doing a media interview on TV, radio/podcasts or even for print/digital stories is not as easy as it looks.

Leave your ego at the door, and be open to doing research, preparation and practice before every major media interview that you do. Yes, the reporter chose to cover your story, but owes you nothing. You have to show up ready, and get them engaged.

To do this right, you must be humble enough to accept media training and feedback.

Media Training Example:
Why CEOs should Always Get Media Training

Before a national TV interview, a former CEO, who had managed hundreds of people, told us, "No, I don't need media training. We will be fine." You can guess how this interview went. Yes, it was a disaster for the history books. The client will remain nameless because our goal is not to embarrass him, but instead to emphasize why you should always get media training or a refresher session before top interviews.

Not only did the client make the mistake of staying up all night, but he also took a hot shower right before the interview that resulted in him sweating so badly that water was dripping off his face — on LIVE national TV. And then, it got worse. He actually picked up his notes — and read them — on LIVE TV. Please don't ever do this!

The good news is that he was finally convinced that media training was needed, and became open to coaching.

Fortunately, I secured another national TV interview for him on *CNN*. To help him prepare for this Sunday interview, we scheduled one-on-one media training on a Saturday via *Zoom*. Together, we worked on his most important soundbites and practiced getting to the point immediately. Because LIVE national TV interviews tend to go very quickly, it's an art to get the key point across as part of a story.

Overall, this second national TV interview was a huge win for him, the host, and producer because he was prepared.

This national live interview aired two times with two teasers over two days. The total airtime was 7 minutes and 20 seconds. **The overall Calculated Publicity Value was $31,400.00.**

To become a Superstar Media Spokesperson, you want to invest in media training.

3 Media Trainer Examples

For our first book, I hired three media trainers for different reasons because it was so important. You've already invested so much time, money and energy in your business or book, so why would you skip this step?

Promoting a brand as a Media Spokesperson is a very different skill compared to writing a book or being an entrepreneur.

Media Trainer 1: As part of my monthly retainer fee for my first dating book Publicist, the agency assigned a Media Coach to videotape me and provide invaluable feedback. We reviewed the mock interview together, and it was beyond helpful. I was really uncomfortable seeing myself on camera at first. But because I was so passionate about getting my message out to the world, I took all of the media training advice I could get.

Media Trainer 2: My second media trainer, Roberta Gale, had done radio for 20+ years. I hired her specifically to help me with radio interviews. She asked for tapes of my radio interviews, and then provided valuable feedback. At the time, I had an ad running in the *Radio-TV Interview Report(RTIR)*, and did coast-to-coast interviews.

Along with improving my radio interview delivery, Roberta recommended a creative topic idea that skyrocketed our PR path. Her suggestion to add movie examples to our key points put us on a success path. Overall, I was fortunate to secure 500+ media interviews over 5+ years for this dating book.

After a few years of promoting this self-published book, I was fortunate to get a literary agent and publisher book deal with *Kensington Books Publishing* in New York City. So you just never know what may come out of your media training.

Media Trainer 3: To promote this new edition, I met my third media trainer, Jess Todtfeld, at the *National Publicity Summit* hosted by Bill and Steve Harrison in New York City. During this summit, authors get two minutes to pitch reporters. And as part of the overall tuition and preparation, authors get one-on-one Media Training with experts.

I felt so lucky to be assigned to Jess Todtfeld because he was a former *ABC, NBC and FOX News Channel* Producer in NYC. Jess provided honest feedback on my Media One Sheet with potential media topics, questions and key soundbites. Overall, Jess took my expertise to a new level, and continues to be one of my top PR mentors today. While *Goody PR* does media training, I have referred clients to Jess to prepare for national media interviews. Yes, it's an investment, but it makes a huge difference.

So as we dig into Media Training Boosters, remember, your first step before any interview is always preparation. Please do not take this step lightly.

It's important to be ready when the lights and the microphones turn to you for insights. You are representing your brand. And no matter how big the media outlet, what you say matters.

Publicity Pro Tip: Don't Skip Your Interview Preparation

When I send a client an interview request and confirmation email, I always include background information about the outlet, host, topic and potential interview questions.

I urge clients to read the interview confirmation and do their homework. However, many clients don't understand the importance of these steps. They are busy running their company, and often just jump into an interview expecting that the reporter is going to do all of the preparation work. This assumption is a huge mistake because the best interviews are two-way conversations.

If you are fortunate enough to get an interview request, your success depends on both you as the guest and the reporter doing their homework.

Along with the host researching your background, you must take a look at the outlet, show, audience, and the interviewer's bio.

To help you look great during media interviews, use our process:

3-Step Interview Success Preparation Tips

Interview Prep Tip 1: Research the Outlet and Show

Interview Prep Tip 2: Research the Host

Interview Prep Tip 3: Review and Practice Potential Questions

If you get an interview, go back to this Media Training Booster chapter as part of your preparation.

For our clients, I will often schedule an interview practice session or prep call via *Zoom* if they have a top media interview —because it's that important. You don't use these skills every day, so take the time to do refresher training.

To provide more context, let's look closer at another example for each of these steps:

Interview Prep Tip 1: Research the Outlet and Show
NPR What's Health Got to Do With It?

For your interview preparation, you can find a lot of information on *Google* and AI about an outlet, show and host. You can also learn more by reviewing their website.

For example, *Goody PR* was fortunate to secure a radio interview on an *NPR* affiliate show for Dr. Laura Gabayan. The media hook was **How to be a Champion for Your Health in 2026** using the Top 3 Wisdom Skills that she scientifically identified in her study and *Common Wisdom* book.

What made this *What's Health Got To Do With It* show a perfect match for her pitch is that the show focuses on helping people navigate the health care system. While the host's medical background was different from Dr. Gabayan, their overall mission to help people better manage their health care is the same.

To help Dr. Gabayan prepare for this top radio interview, I sent her information about the show and host with their website in the Interview Confirmation.

ABOUT THIS NPR SHOW
What's Health Got to Do With It?
Airs on WJCT News 89.9, Jacksonville, FL

What's Health Got to Do with It? is a weekly talk program that airs on Saturdays at 4 PM EST and Sundays at 9 PM EST, and is hosted by Dr. Joe Sirven. This talk show examines where health care intersects with daily life, and helps guide the listeners through an increasingly convoluted medical bureaucracy. These days, health is a lot more than Googling the latest medical breakthrough or seeing your doctor. Staying healthy when you are well and getting healthy when you are sick means knowing how to interact with and navigate an incredibly complex health care system. Owned by *WJCT, Inc.*, it is an *NPR* member station.

In addition to reading about the show, you should LISTEN to one of the episodes to get a sense of the host's style and the format. Some radio and podcast hosts will require pre-interviews so you both show up better prepared.

Interview Prep 2: Research the Host

Host Dr. Joe Sirven, Neurologist

Every show also has a host and/or someone who is going to interview you. Even if you are a celebrity, you should always show up prepared to connect not only with the audience, but also the host.

Remember, you are about to have a CONVERSATION with a reporter who chose to interview you, out of thousands of emails.

Because your interview is earned media coverage versus a paid advertisement, you need to come across as genuine, authentic and prepared.

So share powerful soundbites, and then take a breath so that the reporter can talk too. While this tip may sound silly, I had a client who talked nonstop on a radio interview for six minutes straight for a ten minute interview.

Remember that every reporter, just like you, has feelings, a story and a mission. Interviews are meant to be an engaging two-way conversation versus a speech.

To ensure your interview success, it's important for everyone to feel that it's a win-win experience. You want to share helpful information with their audience, and the reporter wants to look good too.

During your interview, you should thank the host immediately for inviting you to be their guest. Use their first name several times to make your interview more personable. Just like dating, it's not all about you. The more you connect with the host in a dialogue, the better your interview will go.

Let's take a closer look at this *NPR* affiliate Host Dr. Joe Sirven's bio and background that I sent to Dr. Laura Gabayan for her interview preparation.

ABOUT NPR SHOW HOST

Dr. Joe Sirven is a Cuban American bilingual experienced medical journalist, who has served as the chief medical contributor for *NBC Latino*, the English language website for Latinos by *NBC News*. Dr. Sirven is a practicing neurologist who has published extensively on epilepsy and its treatment. He is passionate about medical – education and has edited seven textbooks and is Chair of Education for the *American Academy of Neurology*. In addition, Dr. Joe Sirven directs the Neurology course for *Mayo Medical School*, Florida campus, and for *Dartmouth Medical School, Mayo Florida* campus. He is also a professor at *Arizona State University* where he teaches Science of Health Care Delivery undergraduate and master's students. *What's Health Got to Do with It?* is provided in part by the *American Brain Foundation, Neurelis* and *Rethreaded Inc.*

Interview Prep Tip 3: Review and Practice Potential Questions

The last step in your interview preparation is to review and practice answering potential questions for your specific interview. While you never want to memorize a script, there are specific soundbites and stories that you can think about before your interview. We will discuss how to use storytelling and soundbites in detail later in this chapter.

For this *NPR* interview, I reviewed the five potential questions below with Dr. Laura Gabayan via *Zoom* before her interview because NPR is a top media outlet. Reporters rarely follow the exact questions sent, but I always send a summary to clients.

Potential Interview Questions Example: *NPR*

For Dr. Laura Gabayan Radio Interview

1. Why is it so important today to be a champion of your own health during Open Enrollment Now and in 2026?

2. How can you best navigate health care changes as a champion for your health?

3. How have you been a champion for your own health challenges?

4. Why did you create your wisdom study?

5. Based on your study and *Common Wisdom* book, what are the top 3 wisdom skills every personal health care champion needs?

Please don't just show up for an interview, and expect the host to do all the work. The better you set the stage for interview success, the more likely you will get PR value.

And if the host doesn't ask you exactly what you want to cover, look for opportunities to change the topic as part of the conversation. Politicians do this ALL THE TIME, and so can you.

For example, *Goody PR set up a local TV interview* for a client's new real estate book. The client met the reporter at a house they were showing. They were so excited about this home that both the client and reporter never brought up her book! When I asked why they didn't talk about the book, the producer got really offended. It's not up to them; it's up to the guest to bring up their book or brand.

And don't forget to give one website URL as part of the conversation.

Overall, media interviews are an opportunity to increase your brand awareness, credibility and gain customers. So remember, your main job is to help others with timely tips that are based on whatever you are promoting.

4.2 Be a Great Visual with High-Quality Sound during Interviews

Your next Media Training Booster is all about ensuring you are a great visual. How you present your message and the sound both play a key role in your interview success. Every host wants a great guest who shows up camera-ready with action photos and b-roll video.

And for virtual interviews, you need the best technology and tools to support a smooth delivery and information exchange.

To better prepare you, let's discuss non-verbal and verbal communications. You want to think about the 55/38/7 Communications Model, also known as Mehrabian's Rule. This formula highlights how body language can have the biggest impact on your delivery.

Media Training Tips: 55/38/7 Communications Model

How Body Language Communication Impacts Interviews

Psychologist Albert Mehrabian developed the **55/38/7 Formula** that represents the breakdown of elements contributing to the total impact of your message, which includes:

- **55 percent** of your message is conveyed through body language and facial expressions.

- **38 percent** of your message is conveyed through tone of voice.
- **7 percent** of your message is conveyed through spoken words.

Because you want to connect with the audience emotionally during media interviews, this communications formula is very important to consider.

* * *

So here are some of our top Media Training Tips for your non-verbal communications that contribute to 55 percent of your overall delivery.

Media Training Tips: On-Camera Hair, Makeup and Clothing

Based on my experience doing TV interviews and working with producers, hosts, and clients for 20+ years, I want to emphasize the importance of your hair, makeup and colors.

Hair Styling — For your hair, you know what looks best for you. So don't cut corners. Make that salon appointment and/or get a professional blow dry. You want to feel confident and good on camera. While this step is not always possible for a last minute interview, do the best you can —and ask for help.

Camera-Ready Makeup — For makeup, both women and men need to pay attention to this detail. Everyone has a different skin tone, so go find experts and get advice on what works best for you. Experts say that exaggerated make-up is good for TV because the lights are so bright. What that means is that extra base color, extra blush and eye liner are all great for TV.

If you don't want to pay a professional makeup artist, you can always go to a local department store. Ask for a makeover for free. Most stores are happy to do a makeover, and then try to upsell you their products. *Sephora* also offers makeup appointments with their stylists for a small fee.

What to Wear —For your clothing and colors, I always recommend wearing something that makes you feel great inside as a top rule to increase your confidence. You also want to keep it simple by wearing solid colors. When I spoke to a national TV producer about this topic, they smiled and commented, "Oh yes, wearing solids is so important. We've actually had to buy clothes for guests who show up in something with patterns."

In terms of colors, our media trainers and producers also recommend **"No red, black and white"** for on-camera interviews. Although I've seen many pundits and guests wear these colors lately, I recommend avoiding these three colors if possible.

For women, your best colors are usually bright tones such as fuchsia, pink, electric blue or a vibrant green color. If those colors are not your favorites, wear whatever color makes you feel good inside; just wear solids and avoid red, white and solid black.

For men, your best colors are neutral colors including a baby-blue, dusty brown, tan, olive green and/or light gray shirt. And please, don't wear a hat. People want to see your face.

If you want to wear your brand colors, that can work too. Overall, most TV shows do not like people wearing a company logo because that is more like a paid ad versus earned media coverage for free. While I have seen several clients wear their logo during interviews, don't be surprised if a producer asks you to not to.

Both men and women should also avoid wearing anything that is distracting like big chunky jewelry. You want the audience to focus on what you are saying instead.

In addition to representing your brand, you want to match the style of the show. So please watch the show in advance. In general, wearing something that is considered business casual such as what you would wear to a professional networking event is usually your best approach.

Most shows no longer show men wearing ties. However, if your interview is on a national business TV show such as *CNBC* or *FOX Business*, a tie might be best. If you want to wear a blazer, navy is a better choice than black.

Media Training Tips: On-Camera Body Language

Once you decide what you are going to wear as a visual, you should be feeling good inside — as you would for a first date. You are making a first impression on camera to the world. Because your body language and facial expressions will account for 55 percent of your interview impact, let's get you ready to shine.

Before going into details, I want to recognize that we are all humans who make mistakes. You will not get your interviews perfect every time. Sometimes you might not feel great, but you do the interview anyway. In all scenarios, you can increase your chances of success by using these body language communication tips.

In many ways, you are an actor on camera. Your non-verbal communication should not come across as fake, exaggerated or over-rehearsed, but you should be very aware of its impact.

To help you look great on camera, use these ten body language tips that are based on our personal experience, media training experts, and media training for clients. Read each tip twice because they are all important.

Top 10 Body Language Tips for Media Interviews

1. **Soft Smile before Interview Starts** — Practice smiling with different smiles in front of a mirror. Have a soft smile ready with your mouth closed before the interview starts.

2. **Smile during Interview Opening** — When invited to speak, many professional spokespeople give a bigger smile to come across as more likeable.

3. **Smile while Speaking a Few Times** — While you are speaking, it's best to smile a few times. Smiling is not always easy during an interview, especially if you are talking about a sensitive topic.

4. **Smile when Not Speaking** — During most interviews, you are always on camera. On Live TV and video interviews, remember to use your soft smile if you are not speaking.

5. **Look at the Host for In-Studio Interviews** — For in-person interviews, look at the host, not the camera person. You can also mirror the host. If the host looks forward at the cameras, you can also do it at the same time. Overall, the camera person will find you. Your primary job is to focus on having a great conversation with the host.

6. **Look Interested** — You always want to look interested in what the host is saying, so lean in and act as if you genuinely care. Remember, it's a conversation versus an ad. So practice your eye contact for in-person and virtual interviews. This step can be even more challenging for virtual interviews if you cannot see the host, but you can do it.

7. **Look at the Camera Eye for Virtual Interviews** — For remote interviews via *Zoom*, *Google Meet*, *WebEx* or other software, always look at the camera eye the whole time. Even if you cannot see the host (which often happens on Live TV), pretend that you can see them. If it helps, tape a picture of them next to the camera eye.

8. **Watch Your Body Gestures** — Your body gestures are very important. Avoid crossing your arms, and don't move your hands anywhere near your face. Remember, you are the main visual for a TV or video interview.

   As an example of what not to do, I had a client who waved his hands in front of his face during TV interviews. When I provided feedback, their response was, "that's just the way I communicate." As a general guideline, please keep your hands below your waist, and don't move them around a lot.

9. **Pay Attention to Your Lighting** — Keep in mind that your lighting can have a significant impact on your TV, video and podcast interviews. Invest in a selfie light and practice your lighting in advance for all virtual interviews. If I schedule a top media interview for a client, I often log in a few minutes early to provide feedback on the lighting. Some media experts say, "Lighting is everything," so don't skip this step!

10. **Sit Up with Relaxed Shoulders at Eye Level** — To appear even more confident, make sure to sit up straight, relax your shoulders, and have the camera at eye level.

To expand on the importance of makeup and lighting, here is a behind-the-scenes example.

Media Example: National TV Anchor Makeup and Lighting Adjustment

I was fortunate to work with a reporter on several TV interviews at a local news station. Fortunately, he was hired for a new national TV anchor job. Because I wanted to support him, I watched the new show and taped it several times during the first few weeks. I noticed that he looked really pale and washed out.

Because I had built a great relationship with this anchor, I made a bold move and texted him this feedback. I first congratulated him again on this new show, and then recommended that he talk to the camera team about this lighting issue.

As a result, the anchor texted back a thank you. He said they added more base color for him. Afterwards, he looked much better and I texted him this positive feedback.

Everyone wants to look good on camera, and it's important to be open to feedback.

* * *

While 55 percent of your media message delivery depends on body language, 38 percent depends on tone of voice. Let's take a closer look at what makes your sound high-quality.

5 High Quality Sound Tips for Virtual and In-Person Interviews

What keeps a radio or podcast host up at night is a guest who shows up for an interview on speaker phone with a bad connection —all while driving in their car.

A TV producer's biggest fears for a virtual interview are that you show up with a poor internet connection, bad lighting, low volume, and/or distracting background noises.

Instead, you want to set up your virtual studio for media interview success, remembering these tips:

1. **Find a Quiet Place** — Make sure you are in a quiet place rather than in the car driving on speakerphone with background noise. I've literally locked myself in a room, and gone into the closet to find a quiet space for a live radio interview. Pay attention to your surroundings.

2. **Make Sure You can Hear the Host** — Invest in *AirPods* and/or a professional headset so that you can easily hear the host's questions.

3. **Get a Great Microphone** — Invest in a professional microphone. While there are many options, I recommend a *Blue Yeti*. Ask your friends for suggestions.

4. **Silence Equipment Sounds** — Before your interview starts, make sure to turn off all electronics with sounds. Silence your mobile phone, and turn off all notifications on your computer and tablet to eliminate distractions. This action item is especially important for LIVE TV and radio interviews.

5. **Vary Your Tone of Voice** — Lastly, vary your tone of voice, take pauses and emphasize key points with a little more volume during interviews. This step is not easy, and requires practice. Practice this advanced skill with a Media Trainer and/or film a one-minute video series where you vary your tone at least three times.

Media Examples: 3 Sound Bloopers

While these interview sound tips may sound obvious, here are three media examples of sound bloopers that could have been avoided with better preparation:

1. **National Radio Show Sound Low** — I received a text from a producer after he pre-recorded a national radio interview that

emphasizes the importance of sound quality. He said, "Wish he had a little higher phone quality situation, but it will work." You never want to get this type of feedback from a producer. I quickly acknowledged their concern, and thanked them for doing extra editing to make the sound better.

After this interview was broadcast, I listened to it before saying anything to the client. While it sounded fine to me, their editors probably increased the volume. I also could hear papers being moved around on a desk, which was distracting. You might not realize what gets picked up during a recording, so just try to avoid any distractions.

2. **Computer Notifications during TV Interview** — During a national TV interview for a client, I could hear the spokesperson's computer notifications dinging during important points. I honestly forgot to share the turn off notifications tip with them during media training, which is why I am emphasizing it here so much.

3. **Vary Tone for Long Radio Interviews** — In another case, I had a one-hour radio interview about my *8-Second PR* book tips. Afterwards, the host shared some brutal feedback that made me re-think my delivery. He said, "You spoke at the same level the whole time and really need to learn how to vary your tone." It was a 5AM PST Live interview, and I admit that I did the interview in bed. This was a big mistake because it lowered my energy. I was so grateful that the host shared his observations and really took his advice to heart. Researching, studying the pros and practicing more really helped me improve.

Some of the best radio show hosts who use voice inflection include *NPR* Hosts Terry Gross (*This American Life*) and Ira Glass (*Fresh Air*). Both use an empathetic tone. They are radio legends known to have an authentic voice rather than sounding like a robot. This authenticity is exactly what you want to convey in your voice.

Overall, a high-energy and conversational approach is always considered the best for radio and podcast interviews. For examples, listen to Ryan Seacrest or Casey Kasem.

During our Dr. Laura Gabayan's *PBS* interview about how she used her *Common Wisdom* skills to deal with the aftermath of the Palisades Fire, she actually got teary describing losing her home and community. While I never recommend planning to cry, this was a real and raw moment that was included in her 2.5-minute national interview.

People want to learn from spokespeople who are both human and passionate experts in their fields. Your emotions really impact how your message is received.

Bonus Content: Podcast Tech Interview Tips

For podcast interviews, all of the technical and media training tips above apply.

You want to take a podcast interview as seriously as a national TV interview. So please avoid bad internet connections, get a selfie light, get your hair and makeup done, and have a professional microphone for high quality sound. And always test your technology before an interview.

While these tips also sound obvious, I can't tell you how many clients don't plan ahead. For example, a client had a major podcast interview about her book, where the host asked her to read a section. The guest's lighting was so dark that it made it almost impossible to see her, a situation which was very unfortunate and distracting.

Many hosts have high anxiety about whether you will skip these sound and lighting checks. Podcasts take an average of 20 hours to produce one episode, so please treat every media interview as a top priority. Show up camera-ready and prepared to be a Superstar Media Spokesperson.

4.3 Use Storytelling and Soundbites to Connect Emotionally

You've now built a foundation to be a Superstar Media Spokesperson. You've also decided what you are going to wear, practiced your body language and know how to vary your tone of voice.

Your next step is to deliver your words with impact. While your words are only 7 percent of the overall message context, they play a very important role in your *Google* and AI search results.

Your best bet is to deliver your message through storytelling and soundbites. As I emphasized previously, you want to avoid sounding rehearsed, but there are a few key things you can do to prepare.

When you are interviewed as a guest on a TV, radio or podcast show, the first thing that you always want to do is genuinely thank the host for inviting you. This step helps you connect with the reporter and introduces your tone, delivery and personality to the audience. Bottom line, this is your moment to come across as likeable.

If the audience doesn't have a positive reaction, chances are good that they will stop watching the video and/or change the channel on TV or radio.

Use Empathy and Emphasis Statements in Your Stories

Your next step is using empathy and emphasis statements in your delivery. No matter what story or words you choose, always use these two skills for different reasons.

To express empathy, one of the first things that my media coach told me for my dating book was, "Never say dating is easy, because no one wants to hear that." She added, "Instead, always start with something like, 'dating is hard' or 'this is not easy.'"

You want to come across as relatable, and so admitting that something was challenging for you can be a really strong way to connect with an audience during interviews.

Once you've set the stage with feelings, you can share memorable stories and tips. Throughout your interview, use emphasis statements to highlight the most important points that you want to convey.

An emphasis statement calls more attention to key information. These statements can also improve a listener's retention rate. Focusing your points on 1-3 insights makes your message a lot easier for an audience to remember.

Emphasis Statement Examples

The most important thing to remember is . . .

*If you only walk away from this interview with one thing, remember.
. .*

The top 2 things you should do are . . .

You must remember to . . .

There are 3 key things to remember, including 1, 2 and 3 . . .

* * *

Power of 3s in Your Media Delivery

Because people have short attention spans, talking in threes can be very helpful. This structure gives your interview more focus, and makes it easier for people to follow you.

To help you practice this skill, identify three key points that you want to get across in an interview. Then, no matter what the reporter asks, twist your answers so they are connected to your key points.

Use Empathy, Emphasis and a Short Story for the Best Impact

If you can combine empathy and emphasis statements with a short story, you will strike media gold with the audience. People connect with stories much faster than with facts. Your challenge is to tell a story in a meaningful way in only a few sentences.

Let's take a look at a closer look at a few storytelling examples:

Media Storytelling Example: Eclipse Children's Book Backstory

For the *APO / Eclipse Glasses* publicity campaign, Author Meg Jerit wrote a children's book called *The Moonies: Journey to the Total Solar Eclipse*. The main messages were to educate children about how weather can impact eclipses, and to share the importance of wearing eclipse glasses.

To connect with the audience during Meg's *KXAN NBC Austin, CBS Waco and FOX Weather TV* interviews, she shared the book's backstory. Meg explained that *The Moonies* is based on her real-life experience. Meg shared that she and her father (*American Paper Optics* CEO/Founder John Jerit) did NOT get to see totality during the 2017 Total Solar Eclipse because a massive cloud blocked their view.

Can you imagine being the biggest manufacturer of eclipse glasses, and you didn't get to see the 2017 Total Solar Eclipse because of a cloud?

Meg explained that as a result of this experience she wrote this story to help children understand how weather can impact your eclipse viewing experience. It was also to help set their expectations.

To connect with her audience, the author emphasized feelings during this TV interview. Meg explained, "I just feel like to experience the Total Solar Eclipse as a child would be a pretty amazing experience."

To make *The Moonies* story even more relatable, Meg explained that the main character is a dog named Shadow, who is based on her real-life dog.

In the end of the book, Shadow saves the day by finding a way for everyone to see the eclipse, despite the clouds.

• ◦ •

As a very different story, here is a second media interview example with great soundbites:

> **Media Storytelling Example: Patriot Of the Week on *Newsmax***
>
> **Climbing Mt. Kilimanjaro Without Prescription Glasses**

In another powerful storytelling interview, *Warriors Heart* Command Center COO and U.S. Marine Corps Veteran Michael O'Dell was featured in a Patriot of the Week segment on *Newsmax* on Live TV.

As I've mentioned, *Warriors Heart* is the first and only private and accredited addiction treatment center in the U.S. that exclusively serves military, veterans and first responders struggling with substance abuse, PTSD, and co-occurring issues.

During this inspiring interview, Michael explained that when he climbed Mount Kilimanjaro, it was hard for him to see because he lost his prescription glasses on the plane. As a result, Michael shared that he did this climb one-step-at-a-time, similar to the 12-step recovery process that his team helps warriors follow.

In addition, Michael spoke about the importance of the climb preparation and teamwork that enabled him to reach the summit on July 4th. The climb team's goal was to raise awareness and funds for veteran healing organizations.

When asked about his journey, O'Dell shared this powerful soundbite:

I really had to focus on every single step I was taking, especially on Summit Day, which is the most challenging day. It's dark, and you start at 01 in the morning. And so I couldn't see because it was dark. I couldn't see because I didn't have my glasses.

And that's kind of a testament to just life. Sometimes life is hard, and we have to have support systems around us that help us continue to take one-step-at-a-time.

These moving stories and soundbites are the key to having a memorable interview. You want people to remember your story way after it airs. It's really important to think ahead of time about a short story example — and then get to the point immediately during Live TV interviews.

* * *

Soundbite Secrets

Anyone can tell their story if they have no time limit. However, most TV interviews are 30 seconds –6 minutes. The average TV interview time is about 2 minutes, so that is why short and impactful soundbites are so important.

Your challenge is to get to the point quickly and emotionally connect with short stories.

To get there, you may want to write out the longer story, and then practice telling it with a Media Trainer and/or colleague to identify what is the most important part to share. Ask for honest feedback, and then practice again based on their suggestions.

The media is always looking for soundbites that are 1-2 sentences to play as an introduction or segment teaser. Think about what gets the biggest reaction when you tell your stories, and then use those points as soundbites.

Media Soundbites Example: Rob Schwartz on Bloomberg Radio

To honor his late father Morrie Schwartz (*Tuesdays with Morrie*), his son Rob was interviewed on *Beasley Boston with George Knight* syndicated on *Bloomberg Radio*. Rob shared great soundbites about why he posthumously published *The Wisdom of Morrie* in 2023.

Rob explained that Morrie wrote this book about living and aging joyfully before he got diagnosed with ALS at age 75.

"While still teaching at Brandeis University, Morrie started talking about what it was like to be ill," Rob explained. As a result, *The Boston Globe* did a story that led Ted Koppel at *Nightline* to interview Morrie.

Rob added, **"One of his students (Mitch Albom) saw the episode, and realized his old Professor had a fatal illness. He decided to meet my father to say his goodbyes, but he was so entranced with what my father was saying that he continued to meet him for 14 consecutive weeks. And then he wrote *Tuesdays with Morrie*, and the rest is history"**(17.5+ million books sold.)

Media Soundbites Example: Eclipse Glasses Safety on *Scripps News*

During the weekend before the Monday's 2024 Total Solar Eclipse, *American Paper Optics* Founder John Jerit shared several great soundbites and stories during a LIVE national TV interview on *Scripps News*.

When asked about safety tips for viewing this spectacle in the sky, John shared this advice:

The important thing to remember is that unless you are in the path of totality, you must keep your eclipse glasses on the whole time. Only when the moon completely obscures the sun are you allowed to take your glasses off...

So for those few moments of totality in Dallas and Indianapolis, I get to take my glasses off and you'll witness the most amazing thing you'll ever see. It's like nothing else. <u>It's going to be the most bi-partisan moment of 2024.</u>

The last sentence was probably the most impactful and true during this election year.

Overall, John told two impactful stories, gave great advice tips, and used emphasis statements.

* * *

As we wrap up this chapter, let's take a quick look at a Case Study example of a paid media spokesperson whose lessons learned do a great job summarizing the key points discussed.

Bonus Content: Spokesperson Interview with Captain Laura Einsetler

How to be a Paid Media Spokesperson by News Outlet

To help you better understand what it takes to become a paid media spokesperson, I interviewed Captain Laura Einsetler, who is a Commercial Airline Pilot and Author with decades of flying experience.

As a paid media pundit, Captain Laura is a Superstar Media Spokesperson, who is under contract with a major news outlet. As a go-to TV guest, she is called for last-minute interviews about airplane safety issues and/or related breaking news.

As the author of *Remove Before Flight: Remove Your Fears and Concerns Before Your Next Flight*, she's built a trusted thought leader brand who educates audiences on anything about aviation.

When I asked Captain Laura for advice tips for how to be a paid media spokesperson and the positive impacts of this role, here are her insights:

1. **What are your Top 3 Tips for how to be a great Media Spokesperson?**

   To be a great media spokesperson, you first need to establish yourself as an expert in your field of work. Remember, you are giving both the journalists and the producers quick, sharp and fast information they need while also helping the viewers/ readers understand the topic better.

   Reach out to the producers at the media outlets you want to work with, explain who you are, and what you bring to the table. You can send them a video/pic/bio of you and let them know you have done media work. You will probably work for free at first in order to build your media presence and credibility.

   Sound concise and look professional. Ask for the questions ahead of time and think of 2-3 quick points for each. You never want to "drone on" with media. Use a ring light or pro lights. Have the computer at your eye level as if you are speaking face to face with the viewers, not angled up your nose! Lol.

2. **As an Airline Pilot, Author, and Speaker, how did you become a paid Media Spokesperson?**

   It is a bit of a snowball effect. If you perform well on-camera and/or in the newspapers, it shows that you can clearly convey your expertise and give value as well as entertainment, and then they will keep calling on you.

   Once other media outlets see you, they too want to work with you. Be aware of your contracts or have an IP attorney look things over to make sure you understand and negotiate as needed.

3. **How has becoming a Media Spokesperson changed your life?**

   Becoming a media spokesperson has changed my life in ways I could never have imagined! I feel very humbled and thankful to have the honor to give back. I am able to help represent the industry that I care so deeply about while educating and empowering the media and the viewers.

Being awarded for this work worldwide has been incredible —and I even have gotten back in touch with long lost friends who had seen me on their TVs!

For more information, visit CaptainLaura.com

This chapter has a lot of very information in it. To help you apply these 3 Media Training Boosters, here are your next step Action Items.

STEP 4: Your Media Training Booster Action Items Recap

To help you use these skills, here are your 3 Media Training Booster Action Items. You can increase your media interview impact and results with great visuals, sound quality and storytelling.

4.1 Set Stage for Interview Success

Moving forward, you should prepare for every media interview by researching the outlet, reporter and potential questions in advance to ensure media success. Watch their TV show and/or listen to their podcast.

4.2 Be a Great Visual with High-Quality Sound during Interviews

To get ready for your TV and video interviews, think about what you are going to wear, your body language and how to vary your tone. Set up a quiet interview space with the best technology to enhance your message delivery.

4.3 Use Storytelling and Soundbites to Connect Emotionally

To increase your interview impact, use emphasis statements with three key points. Identify 1-3 short stories and soundbites that make you relatable and memorable.

With these new Media Training Boosters, you are now on the road to becoming a Superstar Media Spokesperson for your business, book, or product.

This advanced skill and education process takes time and practice, so come back to this chapter often and/or hire a Media Trainer to help you.

Never stop believing in the importance of sharing your story and tips with the world! With the right Media Trainers, practice, commitment, empathy, emphasis statements, and tone, you can have an even bigger impact —and make it look easy too!

MEDIA RELATIONS BOOSTER:
Build Long-Term Relationships with Reporters

> This will be an everlasting love.

–This Will Be by Natalie Cole

How can you build long-term media relationships so that a reporter becomes a champion for your brand, book or business? If you can find the right reporter who falls in love with your story, they will keep covering your brand story over and over again. You always want to build on that relationship rather than take it for granted.

Instead of your interview being a one-hit wonder, you want to build win-win media relationships with reporters, assignment managers and/or producers. You ideally want to be recognized as a go-to credible source who gets invited back for future stories.

For our *American Paper Optics* / Eclipse Glasses campaign, *Goody PR* was fortunate to win the *Best Media Relations Campaign– Gold Award* for the *2024 Bulldog PR Awards* that are judged exclusively by journalists.

Let's take a closer look at 3 ways to boost your media relations for long-term success.

STEP 5: Media Relations Boosters

5.1 Be Patient, Persistent and Never Desperate

5.2 Be Reliable, Responsive and Resourceful to Reporters

5.3 Share Sincere Praise and Appreciation

Working with the media is a delicate dance. If you are a publicist, you are in the middle between your client and the reporter. Your job is to connect the dots and make it easier for everyone to tell your client's story. To be successful, you want to send pitches with great content and spokespeople to entertain and/or educate their audience.

And just like any long-term relationship, it can take time to build trust with a reporter.

5.1 Be Patient, Persistent and Never Desperate

Journalists are busier than ever today with nonstop breaking news, so you must use my mantra "be patient and persistent and never desperate" in all interactions.

Whether you are pitching stories via email, phone, or text, you never want to have too many communications in a short timeframe. The only reason to have excessive communications is for a last-minute interview that is within the next 2-24 hours.

Pitch Hot, Warm and Cold Media Leads

Similar to prospecting for sales leads, you want to use different strategies when pitching hot, warm and cold media contacts or leads. Your job is to sell the reporter on your story idea, and most reporters don't say yes the first time you reach out to them.

Because hot and warm leads know you already, reaching out to them first with custom messages and pitches is often the best way to get earned media coverage. Keep a short list of these leads based on their subject area.

For example, Roger Russell, Senior Editor at *Accounting Today*, was on the top of our list to pitch stories for *Tax-Free Wealth* Author, CEO and CPA Tom Wheelwright. While working on Tom's PR for 5+ years, Roger included his tax insights in 22 feature stories. To build on this long-term media relationship, I kept sending Roger timely story ideas and met him in person for lunch in NYC at his office during a business trip. Roger recognized Tom was a credible, go-to source, and it was a win-win relationship.

However, you can also turn your cold contacts into warm or hot leads with the right research and media hook. It just might take a lot more work at first.

Goody PR has been fortunate to secure top media interviews by reaching out to the right reporter at the right time with the right media hook. Reporters are always looking for a new, fresh perspective – so always reach out to journalists who cover your niche, even if you don't know them.

Based on pitching unknown contacts, I've been able to secure thousands of interviews for clients on major outlets, including *CNN, NewsNation, BBC World News, PBS, The Wall Street Journal, Forbes, Fast Company, People Magazine, Psychology Today, The Business Journals, WebMD, NPR, Bloomberg Radio* and many more.

Pitch Hot, Warm and Cold Media Contacts	
Type of Contact	**Description**
Hot Leads	Your hot leads are media contacts, who are passionate about sharing your story with the world. While you still have to pitch them a great story, they have done multiple stories about your brand. They are actively reporting on your subject area, and you are on their expert list.
Warm Leads	Your warm leads are reporters who know about your product and the key benefits. They may have covered you in the past, but it's been some time. They are more likely to share your story, but it may require multiple pitch ideas and follow-up. You need to nurture these media relationships.
Cold Leads	Your cold lead contacts are unfamiliar with your story. You need to generate interest by pitching them a Wow Story with a powerful media hook that gets them to say YES.

You can also ask your personal network and other reporters you know for referrals. By saying that you were referred to a reporter by a specific person can significantly increase your chances of securing media. This approach does not always work, but it's worth a try as long as you have the permission of the other person to use their name.

Be Patient with the Interview Process

In most cases, the bigger the outlet, the longer it may take for an interview to get secured. This long-term lead time is especially true for national TV, print publications, radio shows and top podcasts.

Many potential clients look at our *Goody PR* website Portfolio page, and see national TV interviews. What I often explain is that there is a story behind every one of these media wins, trying to set expectations that it's not as easy as it looks.

What you don't see is all the back-and-forth emails, calls and texts with reporters and clients to make stories happen. It's important to think of your communications with reporters as a delicate dance. You want to pace your communications. Don't call or email too much, and find the best times to pitch and follow-up.

Reporters have short attention spans, like most of us, so it's ok to follow-up a few times.

However, it's very important to be patient, persistent and never desperate, similar to dating. Some clients get it, while others have wishful thinking that lightning will strike during the first month of their contract. While you may get very lucky, it's much more likely that a top media interview will take time, relationship building and a powerful media hook story.

Media Example: Patience with *People Magazine Feature Story*

As an example of a story that required patience, *People Magazine* requested an interview with *APO* CEO/Founder John Jerit on March 22, 2024, which was less than three weeks before the April 8, 2024, Total Solar Eclipse.

While the phone interview was scheduled for Friday, March 22, the reporter asked to move it at the last minute because of breaking news.

Fortunately, this phone interview got moved to Tuesday, March 26, which was about two weeks before the eclipse. The clock was running out fast at this point, and *APO's* media requests were peaking during these final countdown days.

After the call, I sent several follow-ups to this *People Magazine* reporter to thank her and ask about the publication date. She wasn't sure, and said that it was now in her editor's control. The only thing I could really do was emphasize that the timing made the story very relevant over the next two weeks – and then cross fingers and toes.

Fortunately, this feature story was finally published on Saturday, April 6, 2024, which was two days before the Total Solar Eclipse.

While this overall timeframe is not that long for a print publication story, it was really important to get the story published before the Total Solar Eclipse. Otherwise, it wasn't going to be a relevant news story.

Fortunately this follow-up produced a feature story from *People Magazine* about John Jerit and his eclipse glasses company.

As a side note, I scheduled a similar phone interview for John Jerit with a reporter from *The Wall Street Journal*. Despite an interview on March 13, his quotes were cut by the editor for a story published on April 1st. I quickly pitched the reporter another story idea —but it never got approved —and then the eclipse was over.

● ● ●

Let's take a look at another media example where even more patience was required. And the end result was a top media story and award.

Media Example: Regional Emmy ® Award for PBS Backstory

Two-Year Journey from First Pitch to Recognition

As another example of the importance of relentless followup, a *Pioneer PBS* story took two years total from the time of our first pitch to their story winning a *Regional Upper Midwest Emmy ® Award*. This award was for a 20-minute *Pioneer PBS* feature story about a World War II book, *40 Thieves on Saipan* by Co-Authors Joseph Tachovsky and Cynthia Kraack.

This award-winning media example was previously discussed in this book. This expanded case study provides more background on the long lead time and steps involved to provide more perspective.

At the awards ceremony in Minneapolis, I was fortunate to meet the Producer Dana in person, who kept saying, **"I've never met anyone like you who just never gave up!"**

To provide you with the backstory timeline, here is the sequence of events:

First Pitch —My first pitch was an email to Dana in August 2020, over 2 years before this award. Dana responded by saying that she liked the story, but could I please contact her again the following June 2021 (Most people would quit here.) They had just wrapped up their season, and were not considering new stories yet.

Second Pitch —As a result, I created a *Google Calendar* appointment with a reminder and followed up in June 2021. It still took another six months of pitching and planning before Dana and her team finally agreed to film an interview in November 2021. It had already been sixteen months of back-and-forth. Patience was a must.

Media Training —Prior to the author interviews, I provided refresher Media Training for Joseph and Cynthia via Zoom.

Visuals Prep —I also worked with the authors on the Digital Press Kit visuals (photos and videos), which was a treasure hunt. Fortunately, Joseph found the off-limits footlocker of his father, Lt. Frank Tachovosky, in the garage after his passing. It was filled with photos and collectibles that told a great story visually.

In addition, Joseph had just visited the *National Memorial Cemetery of the Pacific*, also known as the *Punchbowl*, in Hawaii for *Veterans Day 2021*. Fortunately, we were able to hire an incredible photographer, Kelli Bullock Hergert, on Oahu to take photos of Joseph paying tribute to the six men from his father's platoon buried there. Joseph placed flower leis, the book, whiskey and rosemary on the graves. These memorable photos were sent to the *PBS* team, and included in their award-winning story.

In-Studio Interview —For the actual interview, Joseph and Cynthia spent the night at a hotel near the *Pioneer PBS* studio that was 2.5 hours from Minneapolis. Dana interviewed them separately and together walking by the lake outside. The entire filming process took about three hours.

Interview Follow-up —After the interview was pre-recorded, I asked for feedback from Joseph and Cynthia first. The next step was to thank the producer profusely and ask if she had a publication date estimate.

Interview Published — It took until the following April 2022 for *Pioneer PBS to* actually air the story, which was also picked up by many local PBS markets.

Emmy ® Nomination —In August 2022, I received a text from the Producer Dana saying:

Your segment was nominated for a Midwest Emmy!!

I was so excited to get this text, and shared it immediately with Joseph and Cynthia. They insisted that we all go together to this ceremony.

Regional Upper Midwest *Emmy* ® Award Ceremony —In October 2022, this Regional *Emmy* ® Award was awarded to the *Pioneer PBS* team in Minneapolis, MN.

To celebrate, everyone involved took turns holding the statue on the red carpet —including the producers, the graphic artist who created illustrations, and authors. I was very grateful to be there, too. It was a very memorable way to celebrate a media win!

Patience, a powerful media hook, the authors dedication (it took Joseph 10 years to write the book), and the *Pioneer PBS* team were all success keys.

* * *

Our goal here is to illustrate why it's so important to build long-term media relationships, never give up, and never be desperate.

5.2 Be Reliable, Responsive and Resourceful to Reporters

While it's mind-boggling to believe, there are people who don't get back to a producer when they get an interview request. Just think about it. A producer is offering to give you free earned media coverage on their network, and the expert chooses not to even acknowledge the request.

As you can imagine, not responding is really bad for your long-term media relations.

Others just don't show up at the scheduled time or are unprepared for media interviews. Every publicist will tell you a horror story about a client who no-showed an interview. It's never intentional, but results in the need for you do a lot of apologizing and begging to get it rescheduled. And while I have been fortunate to get 99% of these interviews rescheduled, it doesn't always get recovered.

In other scenarios, guests show up without knowing anything about the host or show. They expect the reporter to do all of the homework. Please don't do this, unless you are a celebrity (and even then, you should be prepared).

Be Reliable and Responsive

Instead, you want to be a Great Guest or publicity professional, who has a reputation for being reliable and responsive. You want to be known as a go-to source who gets back to reporters in a timely way.

Why You Should Get Back to Reporters ASAP for Interview Requests!

While a major national interview can take months of planning and patience, there are also stories that come up at the last minute. A reporter is often on a tight deadline, and the news cycle can shift as fast as the weather. Keep in mind that producers are constantly under tremendous stress to pull stories together with great guests.

Bonus Content: TV Anchor Insights
GoalChat Live Podcast: Amplifying Your Voice

During a recent *GoalChat Live Podcast* hosted by The Book Proposal Expert Debra Eckerling on 1/26/26, I was fortunate to be a last-minute guest on her "Amplifying Your Voice" themed show.

This panel also included guests Cheryl Tan (Former TV Anchor, and now *Cheryl Tan Media*, who is a Media Trainer and Podcast Show Strategist) and Bobbie Carlton (*Innovation Women/Speaker Platform, Innovation Nights, and Carlton PR & Marketing.*)

Based on extensive TV experience, Cheryl Tan emphasized, "Say yes to opportunity, especially if it comes in the form of a media interview."

Cheryl went on to explain that years ago she was assigned a feature story about a local business. When she selected the small business and reached out to schedule the TV interview, the owner said, "No, I really can't do it today. I'm not ready. I have to get my hair done." (Ok, I get the importance of looking good on camera, but . . .)

Cheryl had to remind her, "I may not be able to return on another day. Story priorities change very quickly."

Your job as a media spokesperson or public relations professional is to make it easy for a producer by responding to interview requests right away. Obviously, if they want you to comment on a news story that doesn't interest you, it's ok to pass —but at least respond.

Goody PR Response Rules for Top Media Interviews

For our *Goody PR* clients, if an outlet requests a TV interview in response to a pitch, I make it our top priority to get it confirmed ASAP. Because TV is the most competitive medium to secure, I immediately start calling and texting the client until I reach someone. I don't want anyone else to get the timeslot, and schedules often change.

News cycles move at warp speed today. If you blink, you can miss a media opportunity. For my dating book, I missed a national TV interview request by one hour. I was at a coffee meeting, and the caller ID was blocked. By the time I called back, they had found another expert for their segment.

To make sure that our clients do not miss an opportunity, *Goody PR* has a 1-hour rule to get a Yes or No response to a reporter for a TV interview request. Yes, this makes our agency look reliable, but what is more important is that I sincerely want the client to get the interview. While sometimes things can be rescheduled to another date, it is rare.

If the client is in an important meeting, I often will tell the producer that I am checking and will let them know Yes or No by a certain time. This update approach can work, and acknowledges that you got their interview request.

If you are a PR professional or potential guest, last-minute interview scheduling can be very stressful. However, if you really want to get top media coverage, being ready at a moment's notice can advance your brand story much faster.

Remember, the reporter chose your story out of hundreds of competitors and pitches —and they are offering to cover your story —for FREE.

As a media example, our client got very lucky that a timeslot on a top local news outlet was still available when their schedule changed.

Media Example: FOX 5 DC: Good Day Morning Show
Only One TV Interview Time Slot Available

When I pitched *FOX 5 DC's Good Day* morning show producer in Washington D.C. (which is the 8th largest Media Market in the U.S.), the client was not available during the only timeslot available due to a meeting conflict. It was a timely story about *Warriors Heart Virginia's* new documentary with *Warriors Heart's* CEO/Founder Josh Lannon and President/Founder and Master Sergeant (ret) Tom Spooner as the spokespeople.

When I asked the producer if they could do it on another day or time, the response was, "No, we have no slots other than Wednesday for the morning show."

Because the client's meeting was very important, they chose to give up this TV interview opportunity. When this type of conflict happens, it always pains me, but it's ultimately up to the client to decide if they want to pass.

Fortunately, in this case, the client's important meeting got moved the next day, and they were now available during the only time slot available.

And fortunately, that one time slot was still available. This LIVE TV interview was in the studio for over five minutes. And even better, the story got republished by *Yahoo! News* and *MSN* – resulting in a 2.7 million total reach for one interview.

The Calculated Publicity Value was $25,500 for the TV interview alone based on a *Nielsen Media Report*.

The most important thing for your long-term media relations is to get back to the producer in a timely manner. Simply by responding, they are more likely to call you next time.

And if you can make it work, one top media interview can be a gamechanger.

Media Availability Example: 3 AM PST Interview
Robert Kiyosaki (*Rich Dad Poor Dad*) and Advisors

To provide insights to spokespeople and marketing teams, I published a video short on our *Goody PR YouTube Channel* about why you should always say YES to an interview, even if it is at 3 AM.

While that time is an extreme example, it can easily happen because of time zone differences. If you are on the west coast or in Hawaii, be open to getting up early for east coast interviews.

This example goes for publicists too because you always want to be there to support clients with LIVE TV interviews. Producers can change the interview time at the last-minute or cancel completely if there is breaking news.

When I booked Robert Kiyosaki (*Rich Dad Poor Dad*) on *FOX and Friends* with four of his Rich Dad Advisors about How to Start Your Own Company and their new book, *More Important Than Money: An Entrepreneur's Team*, I was up at 3 AM PST to make sure everything ran smoothly.

Fortunately, there was no breaking news, and it was a 6.5 minute interview. Everyone was able to share two entrepreneur tips. To make this interview happen, I got input from each of the interviewees and drafted a script. The producers were hesitant to have so many guests in one interview, but with this Q and A as a guide, the story got approved.

This interview was a major media win and worth all of the extra efforts behind the scenes.

The Calculated Publicity Value for this media interview was $136,000, according to Nielsen Media Reports. It was definitely worth getting up early.

In a best-case scenario, you do such a great job on your first interview that the producer invites you and/or your client back for repeat interviews. A reporter would much rather call someone who they know will show up and deliver great content versus an unknown.

Media Relations Success: Repeat Request by *Scripps News* TONIGHT

How a CEO got invited back for Last-Minute Interview

As a media relations success story, a national *Scripps News* TV producer called us because they wanted our client as a repeat guest that evening. As a result, I immediately shifted gears to contact the client and respond.

To get an answer quickly, I called and texted the thought leader Alan Crone. Because he is an Employment Law Attorney, CEO/Founder of *The Crone Law Firm* and Author of *The Law at Work*, they wanted him to do a *Labor Day* weekend interview about the meaning of the holiday.

When Alan did not answer his phone, I called and texted his Executive Assistant, Marketing Manager and local Memphis Publicist until I got an answer.

Fortunately, Alan was available and happy to do this interview that was a perfect match for his background and brand. During this LIVE TV interview, Alan explained the history of Labor Day, why employee rights are important in America, overtime issues, tips for resolving workplace issues, and why he believes that 90 percent of workplace issues are caused by communication issues.

This repeat guest request is a great example of how media relations can benefit you.

* * *

In addition to being reliable and responsive, you want to be resourceful with reporters.

Be Resourceful

Providing reporters with reminders, data and visuals can also strengthen your media relationships.

Bonus Content: Media Relations Insights from *KSAT ABC News* Reporter

When I interviewed former *KSAT ABC News* San Antonio Reporter Jonathan Cotto for this book, I asked what helped him the most when I pitched stories. As I mentioned in the Media Outreach Booster chapter, Jonathan covered multiple client stories over three years. This type of media relationship is priceless for any PR agency or spokesperson.

Jonathan emphasized, ***Because I was running around to different locations and often covering 3-4 stories every day, I loved that we had a media relationship where you could text me reminders saying — I sent you a pitch email —and then include a little teaser about the topic. I always appreciated that so much, and it reminded me to pitch your story to my producer.*** By doing homework for a reporter, you may be able to fast-track an interview. Remember, they are under tremendous pressure with limited time, so the more resources with references with credible sources that you can provide them, the better.

Here are a few examples of helpful resources that you can provide journalists:

5 Types of Media Resources

1. Provide a Q and A in your pitch with short answers to each question. Include specific examples and unique tips based on your personal experience and insights.

2. Provide a short one-paragraph bio about expert guests. Include their job title and location in the first sentence.

3. Share recent studies that can support your story, and include a reference link to the exact source so they can easily fact-check your information.

4. Provide helpful statistics with a credible source. Do not use AI as a reference without quoting the specific source with a direct link. For example, *NIH, CDC* or *Johns Hopkins University* are all recognized as credible sources for health and wellness stories.

5. Provide a Digital Press Kit on a *Google Drive* with potential visuals. Have we emphasized this tip enough? Most TV stories are visual based, so this is a must-have.

And after a phone interview for a print story, a reporter may have follow-up questions. If they send you additional questions, make sure you reply with answers within 24 hours. You are building media relations, so provide a prompt response.

You want to get this type of reply from a reporter:

This is great, thanks! I'll be sure to update you if I hear anything about the publication date. You are so thorough. –Crystal

Remember, media relations is just like dating; you always want to build a long-term relationship. For the publication above, I've been fortunate to have this military publication write five feature stories over five years for different clients.

5.3 Share Sincere Praise and Appreciation

The last action item for you in this Media Relations Booster chapter is to always send a sincere thank you to reporters and their support team for their work. Include in your thank you specific things that the reporter did to go above-and-beyond.

As we've discussed, reporters prefer to work with people they like. Always show appreciation for their work —every step of the way. Remember, they chose your story out of thousands of emails and pitches. You are paying them nothing for earned media coverage.

We especially like to thank the producer, anchor, host, graphic artists, digital team and really anyone involved in making a story happen. In your thank you emails and texts, point out the little details they did when sharing your story with the world.

For example, they may have included your visuals, added your phone number in a banner, and/or linked directly to your website in their online write-up. Every TV interview does not get posted online, so thank them if they took the time to publish a recap.

Reporters don't have do any of these extra steps. They are telling your story at no charge, so go out of your way to be grateful and build invaluable media relationships.

To give you a better idea of what you might say, below are three examples of thank you emails that I've sent after a story was published with specific praise:

3 Media Thank Yous Mention the Details

WOW, WOW and WOW! Thank you so much for your KATU ABC 2 interview today with our PR client on your morning show. Helen asked so many great questions, and the graphics looked great. I sent the interview link to X and his entire team, and have been sharing it all over social media.

Thank you again for interviewing American Paper Optics CEO John Jerit on NewsNation about Real vs. Fake eclipse glasses in prep for the April 8, 2024, Total Solar Eclipse. I especially loved your dog wearing eclipse glasses, too.

Wow! Thank you so much for your feature story in GOBankingRates with Rich Dad Advisor and TENERO Financial Education YouTube Channel Host/Founder Garrett Z. Sutton that was published yesterday. I love how you pulled his 5 tips together, and really appreciate you linking to TENERO in the opening paragraph.

Along with being a grateful human-being, you always want to build long-term media relations with reporters. Let's look at some examples of repeat interviews:

How to Manage Long-Term Media Relationships

Media relations are especially important for your brand's success. If you find a reporter who writes for your ideal audience and wants to do a feature story about you, do a dance! You just won the media lottery!

One of our PR colleagues Susan Bejeckian (*Bejeckian PR*) specializes in travel PR. With decades of experience representing top hotels and destinations in the Solomon Islands and Fiji, Susan has built solid media relationships with travel writers. As a result, her clients have gotten multiple stories in *Travel + Leisure, National Geographic, Los Angeles Times* and many more national and local publications.

Let's look at another long-term media relationship example :

Media Relations Example:
Connecting Vets covered 9 Stories over 2 Years

If you find a reporter who loves writing stories about you and/or your client, treasure this contact. These media relationships happen when all the stars line up.

I've been fortunate to build a long-term media relationship with a reporter for *Connecting Vets*, which is a national outlet covering veteran topics. This publication was a perfect match for *Warriors Heart's* recovery program that is exclusively for military, veterans and first responders.

To make things really easy for this journalist, I provided direct quotes from the spokesperson(s) in a Q and A format with a press release and media images.

Fortunately, this reporter decided to turn nine of our pitches into national news stories that were picked up by *Google News* over two years —without doing an interview. Because time is so valuable today, this process worked great.

This reporter is also an incredible writer, which added to high-quality coverage. Of course, every step of the way, I thanked this reporter profusely for the stories and their support of *Warriors Heart.*

As a general guideline, you always want to treat your media relations like gold and stay in touch with the reporters who are your hot leads. You want to nurture these relationships by being positive and supportive. If they ask for help finding a guest, jump to help them, even if it's not for your client.

Media Relations Example:
Helped *NewsNation* Producer Find Guest

As an example of how to build long-term media relations, a *NewsNation* producer called me on a Saturday afternoon desperately seeking a marketing spokesperson. They wanted to do a LIVE national interview in a few hours and needed a media expert to comment on the *Bud Light* backlash that blew up on social media.

Because I was not the right person, I brainstormed with PR friends. Fortunately, through a PR networking group, I found the perfect person for them to interview.

What I did not realize at the time that I referred this spokesperson was that she had NO media training. To make everyone look good, I provided her with last-minute media training tips via *Zoom* before her 5 PM LIVE national TV interview.

Overall, she did a terrific job during the interview. Afterwards, she wrote an awesome testimonial for me.

Most people might say that dropping everything on a Saturday afternoon for a story that was not for my clients was really going above-and-beyond. Yes, that is true —but that producer is now my go-to person at this national TV outlet.

＊ ＠ ＊

Along with giving praise and helping reporters find guests when needed, you can interact with many journalists now on social media. To show your appreciation for their coverage, make sure to share their stories online and tag them.

Media Relations Tip: Share Your Media Coverage Within 48 Hours

If you or your company is fortunate enough to get an earned media story, you should share it online the same day.

Remember, you won the media lottery when the reporter chose to cover your story out of the hundreds, if not thousands, of daily email pitches. While immediate social media sharing may sound like common sense, many people wait or forget completely.

Bonus Content:
Social Media Post Insights from *KSAT ABC News* Reporter

When I asked former *KSAT ABC News* TV reporter Jonathan Cotto for his opinion on how quickly someone should post a media story online, he replied, "Sharing the story within two days is best. If it is evergreen, share when you can at your convenience."

Jonathan then added, "I absolutely loved it when you shared a story that I did about the eclipse, and the impact of the – story, and then I re-shared it as well."

Keep in mind that reporters are under tremendous pressure not only to produce great content, but to get eyeballs on their stories. The best way that you can thank them is to post their story and tag them. They covered your story for FREE (and 99% of the time, it's positive press.) How much does it cost you to share it online? Nothing, so just do it!

And if a reporter leaves a job, make sure to congratulate them, follow their career moves, and stay in touch!

Media Relations Example:
Follow Reporter's Career Changes

You always want to follow a reporter's career changes. You've built a relationship with a person, and so you want to congratulate them on new jobs.

For example, after working with *FOX 11 Los Angeles* on many stories, one of their top reporters, Elex Michaelson, got a new anchor job and new 2-hour show on *CNN*.

It is a nightly show called *The Story Is with Elex Michaelson* that features international and California topics. In addition, a top producer from *FOX 11 Los Angeles* got hired by *CNN* to produce stories for this new show.

When Elex left *FOX 11 Los Angeles*, I posted a thank you video that highlighted seven stories that he had done for our *Goody PR* clients over the years.

When you find a media rockstar like Elex, build on that long-term media relationship through sincere praise via texts, comments and shares.

* * *

Can you give Gifts to Reporters?

Lastly, consider different ways to thank a reporter. Everyone likes to be appreciated and supported. Genuine appreciation can go a really long way. While your gut instinct may be to send flowers or a *Starbucks* gift card, reporters are not really supposed to accept gifts.

However, what I've found is that you can give them a relevant gift, which may include an autographed copy of your book, branded merchandise and/or sample products.

For many local TV interviews connected to food or travel, the reporters are usually happy to accept samples. For example, our travel PR colleague Susan Bejeckian (*Bejeckian PR*) has secured stories on *KTLA* for several years about the Annual Lavender Festival in Lompoc, California. The anchors love getting samples of their soaps, oils, sachets and more.

You can also mail a reporter your product and/or branded merchandise. For our eclipse glasses campaign, the *American Paper Optics* CMO often mailed a gift package to reporters if there was enough advance notice. This campaign moved so fast that sometimes it was a same-day TV interview. In several cases, the reporters actually wore the *APO* eclipse glasses on-air, which was a priceless visual.

You can also ask a reporter if they have time for coffee or lunch —if you are fortunate enough to live in the same city or visiting. Their time is so valuable that this one-on-one request may be impossible to schedule. Instead, it may be easier to meet them at a local conference or press awards.

As key takeaways for this chapter, let's take a quick look at what you've learned and how to apply these 3 Media Relations Booster Action Items.

STEP 5: Your Media Relations Booster Action Items Recap

To help you apply these Step 5 skills, here are your 3 Media Relations Booster Action Items for your long-term success.

5.1 Be Patient, Persistent and Never Desperate

Create a list of your Hot, Warm and Cold Media Leads, and pitch them differently to build long-term media relations. While you always want to be patient with reporters, you must follow-up in a timely manner. It's a delicate balance, so view each relationship differently. If it makes sense, add your reporter follow-up action items to a *Google Calendar* with reminders.

5.2 Be Reliable, Responsive and Resourceful to Reporters

Set best practices for you and/or your client for how fast you plan to get back to a reporter who requests an interview. Remember, if you blink by waiting a few hours to reply, they may give your TV interview to someone else. Build your credibility by providing great guests, credible data and high-quality visuals to journalists.

5.3 Share Sincere Praise and Appreciation

Always write sincere and specific thank you emails and texts to reporters who cover your story, no matter how big the outlet. People appreciate being thanked for their hard work, and it can help you build invaluable media relationships.

You now have the tools and insider secrets for how to build long-term media relations with reporters, so they keep covering your stories. Please make these advice tips part of your best practices process to ensure your publicity success.

Remember, you want these media relationships to have the same mutual respect as an "everlasting love."

As a side note, I was very fortunate to thank Natalie Cole in person on a flight from Austin, Texas, back to Los Angeles. She was the keynote speaker at an addiction conference that I attended with a client that day. We just happened to be on the same plane that evening. Her talk made an incredible impression on me. She was so kind, sincere and authentic.

You always want to be remembered for being genuine and grateful. People will remember how you make them feel, especially people in the media.

PART 3

MAGNIFY AND MEASURE WINS

Make your story go viral with Digital Marketing, Book Marketing and Top Media Boosters.

Measure your media and business wins.

DIGITAL MARKETING BOOSTER:
Reach Millions with Online Strategy, Video and AI

Our hearts were ringin'
In the key that our souls were singin'
As we danced in the night, remember
How the stars stole the night away, oh, yeah

-*September* by Earth, Wind & Fire

If you are doing a Publicity Campaign and/or Public Relations Program, you must have a digital marketing strategy to magnify your story to millions of potential fans. I've stopped counting the number of potential clients who tell me —

- We don't need your help with social media.
- I am going to do my own social media.
- I don't have time to bother with social media.

Why would you spend valuable time and invest in a product, writing a book, or running a company —and not budget for digital marketing? You CANNOT skip this step.

To build loyal fans, credibility, and influence, you MUST create an online marketing strategy that aligns with your overall mission, goals and brand.

And if you need to learn social media basics, read our step-by-step chapter in *8-Second PR* and/or other how-to books such as *The Social Shift* by Katie Brinkley.

Similar to media coverage, you want to post compelling social media content that connects emotionally with your ideal target audience.

The song for this chapter is *Come and Get Your Love* by *Redbone* because you want to organically attract followers online. You want people to follow you on *Facebook, Instagram, YouTube, TikTok, LinkedIn*, and other platforms because you are posting creative content that engages them.

You want your followers to have a positive feeling about your content, so they make your story go viral through social sharing.

As an extra booster, this chapter includes how to develop a big picture Digital Marketing Strategy, use video marketing and how AI can make your efforts more efficient.

STEP 6: Digital Marketing Boosters

6.1 Define Your Digital Marketing Strategy and Top 3 Platforms

6.2 Produce Video Storytelling Content that Educates and Entertains

6.3 Use AI to Maximize Digital Marketing and PR Efficiencies

It's important to mention that while a reporter does not always consider your number of followers when deciding whom to interview, it can help you stand out among your competition. And if you're an author who wants to get a literary agent and/or a publisher, you will never get one without a digital platform.

To help you get started on your Digital Marketing Boosters, here are some insider tips.

6.1 Define Your Digital Marketing Strategy and Top 3 Platforms

Many brands, small businesses, thought leaders and authors do not prioritize this critical Digital Marketing Booster in their big-picture strategy. Ultimately, your plan should identify your top three social media platforms so you can focus your efforts where it will have the biggest impact.

Big-Picture Digital Marketing Strategy

To amplify you story to a broader audience, you need a Digital Marketing Strategy that is in alignment with your Public Relations Program, campaign objectives and overall business goals.

Your strategy should include a content calendar to regularly post images, video and stories that showcase your brand. Similar to media coverage, your posts should entertain and educate followers. Tell powerful stories, share educational tips, and extend your media coverage reach in your posts.

As a foundation, here are eight core elements that you should include in your plan:

8 Digital Marketing Strategy Elements

1. **Clear and Measurable Goals:** Define specific digital marketing goals, which may include increased awareness, engagement, and sales by X amount.

2. **Identify Your Target Audience:** Define your target audience's demographics, which may include their age, income, geography, pain points, personalities and more.

3. **Define Your Platforms:** Pick your top three social media channels to focus your efforts. Build your brand following with consistent and authentic content that connects.

4. **Define a Content Strategy:** Define your core brand messages, main stories, content format, and how you will use AI to improve efficiencies.

5. **Create a Content Calendar:** Create a detailed content calendar based on how often you want to post. And identify what days and times are best to reach your audience.

6. **Identify Key Calendar Dates:** Identify national months and days that can be connected to your posts. For example, *World Kindness Day, Mental Health Awareness Month*, and *Entrepreneur Month* may be important for your brand.

7. **Use Social Media Management Tools:** To maximize your results and efficiency, use social media management tools to schedule and manage your posts. Some tools have a monthly fee, while others are free. Consider using top social media management tools, including *Buffer, Hootsuite, Sprout Social, and Hubspot.* Use *Google* to find the latest tools, prices and request a demonstration.

8. **Identify Metrics for Measuring ROI:** Determine how you will measure your digital marketing results and Return on Investment (ROI). Views, Followers, Engagement, Sentiment, Comments, Shares and Subscribers are all important metrics to track. Many social media platforms have been updated to include an Insights page. Paid tools can provide you with a more sophisticated analysis.

Your digital marketing strategy needs to go way beyond randomly posting stuff. Instead, you want fans to FALL IN LOVE with your brand, and recognize you as a go-to source for your subject area.

Before doing anything, draft your digital marketing strategy. Review it with your marketing and PR teams, and get honest feedback and suggestions. For example, for our *APO* / Eclipse Glasses campaign, we met regularly with their CMO and external digital marketing team (*Bazztiki Digital*). Based on our Public Relations Program strategy, we identified key dates and milestones together, so we were all in sync.

To help you better understand how to create a big picture digital marketing strategy and approach, here are first-hand observations on the *APO* / Eclipse Glasses campaign:

Bonus Content: Insights from *Bazztiki Digital Founder*

***APO* Eclipse Glasses Digital Marketing Success Strategy**

To provide you with more insights on the *APO / Eclipse Glasses* digital marketing strategy, Winston Bromley, *Bazztiki Digital* Founder (whose team managed this part of the campaign), shared the following points:

One of the key drivers behind the rapid success of APO's Eclipse Glasses digital campaign was strong, timely content that answered common questions, followed trends, and emphasized buying safely direct from APO.

We launched a daily storytelling-based content strategy focused on three themes, with safety quickly becoming the breakout topic.

At the time, low-quality eclipse glasses were flooding the market, creating real consumer risk and an opportunity for us to lead with education and trust.

Working closely with the team, we produced short-form videos with diverse spokespeople and trend-driven formats to reach our target audiences. This content not only encouraged engagement, but also helped news outlets better understand and amplify APO's story, often referencing insights directly from our videos.

*   ●   *

With the big picture strategy in mind, let's now look at the best ways to focus your energy.

Identify Your Top 3 Social Media Platforms

With this big-picture foundation, your next step is to choose your top 3 social media platforms for your brand, business or book. Because you want to be smart and strategic, identify your best social media platforms based on data and trends.

Think about where your target audience lives online. And to help you make these really important decisions, let's take a closer look at digital marketing trends and numbers.

Top Social Media Platforms:
Pew Research Center

According to *Pew Research Center* (September 2025), **over half or 53 percent of U.S. adults "say they at least sometimes get news from social media."**

So if you're not sharing and re-posting your news stories on social media, you are missing out on a huge opportunity to reach millions of potential fans, clients and/or customers. If an outlet has a lower circulation, you can significantly boost your reach by sharing it on social media.

In this report, *Pew Research Center* **explains the top social media platforms where adults consume news include:**

- *Facebook* (38%)
- *YouTube* (35%)
- *Instagram* (20%)
- *TikTok* (20%)
- *X,* **formerly known as** *Twitter* **(12%)**

While *Pew Research Center* reports that the top platforms where adults consume news on social media are *Facebook* and *YouTube*, you also have to look at the core demographics and behaviors for each platform.

Where Is Your Audience Online?

Demographics for Most Popular Social Media Platforms

Let's take a closer look at the top platforms, age ranges, behaviors and a case study example to give you digital marketing strategy ideas for your brand.

If your core demographic is 25-34, you are in luck because that is the top age range using social media in the United States. However, you'll find information on where users spend most of their time in age ranges between 18-65+ by doing your research.

SproutSocial is a top social media management platform that studies these demographics for you. Let's look at this data to identify your top three platforms.

Top Social Media Platforms: *Demographics and Usage*

Why Social Sharing for Your Publicity Is So Important

According to *SproutSocial's* 2025 demographics report, below is the breakdown of social media usage by age range and platform in the United States:

- 18-29 yr: *YouTube (93%), Instagram (76%), Facebook (68%), Snapchat (65%)*
- 30-49 yr: *YouTube (94%), Facebook (78%), Instagram (66%), Pinterest (43%)*
- 50-64 yr: *YouTube (86%), Facebook (70%), Instagram (36%), LinkedIn (30%)*
- 65+: *YouTube (65%), Facebook (59%), Pinterest (22%), Instagram (19%)*

* * *

If you dig deeper into this report, you can find more information about the demographics, behaviors, and average time spent for each social media platform:

Facebook demographics and usage

- Number of monthly active users: 3.065 billion

- Largest age group: 25-34 (31%)
- Gender distribution: 43.2% female, 56.8% male
- Time spent per day: 32 minutes

YouTube demographics and usage

- Number of monthly active users: 2.504 billion
- Largest age group: 25-34 (21.7%)
- Gender distribution: 46% female, 54% male
- Time spent per day: 49 minutes

Instagram demographics and usage

- Number of monthly active users: 2 billion
- Largest age group: 18-24 (31.7%)
- Gender distribution: 49.4% female, 50.6% male
- Time spent per day: 32 minutes

TikTok demographics and usage

- Number of monthly active users: 2 billion
- Largest age group: 25-34 (35.3%)
- Gender distribution: 44.3% female, 55.7% male
- Time spent per day: 47 minutes

LinkedIn demographics and usage

- Number of members: 1 billion
- Largest age group: 25-34 (50.6%)
- Gender distribution: 43.6% female, 56.4% male
- Average visit duration: 11 minutes and 19 seconds

SOURCE:
SproutSocial (Feb 24, 2025)
Social media demographics to inform your 2025 strategy

After reviewing this data, identify your top 3 social media platforms based on what is best to reach your audience online.

As an example, here is case study that may help you choose:

Case Study Example: Top 3 Platforms for *Goody Business Book Awards*

As background, our *Goody PR* agency runs the *Annual Goody Business Book Awards* program to recognize social impact authors who are making a difference with words. These authors tend to be thought leaders who are further along in their career. Because their nonfiction, self-help books are often based on years of experience, the core demographic for these book awards tends to be a little older.

To create a digital marketing strategy and content, the team includes *Mary Rau Public Relations Inc.* Our Web Manager and Honorary Board of Advisors, who are all media and marketing experts, also provide input and engagement.

Fortunately, hundreds of authors, publishers, publicists, agents, and fans nominate their books in 1-50 categories every year on GoodyBusinessBookAwards.com.

Based on our research, experience and target market, our social media focuses on these three platforms:

1. ***Instagram* and *Facebook* *@goodybusinessbookawards*** — Author-themed content is posted primarily Monday-Friday based on the platform's Insights. Every *Instagram* post is automatically shared on our *Facebook* page. Most of the engagement with authors is on *Instagram* versus *Facebook*.

2. ***YouTube.com/GoodyPR*** —Our team regularly posts short videos on a *Goody Business Book Awards* Playlist on *Goody PR's YouTube Channel* using keyword phrases such as "business book awards" to increase SEO.

3. ***LinkedIn*** —While content is posted less frequently on *LinkedIn*, it is the largest professional networking platform. Thought leaders and authors are much more likely to post about their career milestones and books on *LinkedIn*.

Overall, the volume of *Goody Business Book Awards* content increases as the final deadline of September 30 for nominations approaches. About 60 percent of the nominations for the whole year are submitted during the final two months.

A second digital marketing campaign starts when the Winners and Finalists are announced by November 15th. For this campaign, our social media team posts the authors and their books for each of the 50 categories over several months.

* * *

Let's break this digital marketing strategy down further with examples to give you helpful ideas:

Content Types: The three types of content posted regularly by the *Goody Business Book Awards* include social media posts (Reels, Stories, Photos, and Ads), Videos (*YouTube* and *Instagram*) and News/Blogs (Press Releases and Blog posts).

Target Market: For this business book awards program, our target audience is primarily 35-65+ nonfiction authors and thought leaders. They are writing about real-life experiences and lessons learned. Most of these authors are small-business owners, professionals, thought leaders, investors, doctors, and more. And while they may have corporate experience, they might be a consultant, trainer or coach now.

To gain insights on your fans, go to your *Facebook* and *Instagram* page's Professional Dashboard, and then click on Audience to see more details.

Below are the Audience Demographics for *Goody Business Book Awards*, which match our goal to reach primarily a 35-65+ audience.

Goody Business Book Awards – Facebook Age Demographics

55-64 = 39.4%
65+ = 23%
45-54 = 16.3%
35-44 = 14%
25-34 = 5.5%
18-24 = 1.8%

Instagram's demographics are pretty consistent, but a little younger, which is in sync with the overall platform.

Goody Business Book Awards – Instagram Age Demographics

45-54 = 27.2%
55-64 = 23.1%
65+ = 18.6%
35-44 = 18.3%
25-34 = 9.5%
18-24 = 3.2%

To provide insights on whether our book awards social media approach is working, we survey all nominees by asking the key question: *Where did you hear about us?* For our first year, we made the mistake of not doing this customer survey. Please don't skip this step because it can tell you what is working best for attracting customers.

Below are the survey results from our *Goody Business Book Awards* 2025 nominees. Because Search/Google/AI is the number one way users find us, this feedback highlights the importance of regularly publishing new content to boost our SEO.

User Survey Results Example
Where did you hear about *Goody Business Book Awards?*

33% = Search/Google/AI (connects to blogs, social sharing and videos)

32% = Publisher/Agent/Publicist/Editor (connects to key target audience)

16% = Friend (connects to social media and word-of-mouth marketing)

9% = Social Media (builds community, reputation and buzz)

3% = News/Blog (contributes to SEO based on website and media)

3% = Previous Winner/ Nominee

4% = Other

To extend the reach of *Goody Business Book Awards*, we provide authors with awards seals, personalized trophies, and customized banners.

As the *Goody Business Book Awards* SEO has grown online, there has been a 10-30 percent increase in nominations per year over the past four years. Along with regular strategy meetings, our team has an annual debrief session to review overall results and brainstorm ways to enhance the program.

If you are an author, or know an author who deserves recognition, consider nominating their books on our website: GoodyBusinessBookAwards.com.

6.2 Produce Video Storytelling Content that Educates and Entertains

Because video is now dominating social media content, this section focuses on video storytelling tips. Our *8-Second PR* book covers social media more broadly. This new *Award-Winning Publicity* book focuses more on the power of video marketing that continues to grow online.

Around 82 percent of internet traffic will be video by 2026, with users spending an average of 100 minutes per day watching online videos, proving that video is no longer just an add-on but the backbone of digital marketing.

Source: *DemandSage*

To help you magnify your publicity, use video to reach millions through authentic and timely content. Videos can have a very positive impact on sentiment by humanizing your brand. People want to buy more from a person versus a brand. As a result, storytelling content is a must.

Just like being interviewed on TV, you want to create videos that both educate and entertain your audience with a unique story and/or insider tips. This storytelling approach is also the fastest way to gain followers and build buzz online.

According to *Wyzowl's State of Video Marketing* report, "The vast majority of people have watched an explainer video about a product."

You can also send your videos to TV and radio reporters who want to see if you are a good media spokesperson.

While you are beyond proud of your business, book or brand, be more creative in posts. For example, share your story-behind-the-story. Post relatable and inspiring stories on your social media, blogs, press releases, and videos. And add humor, if appropriate.

When creating your videos, consider posting in these five formats for different reasons:

Top 5 Video Content Trends and Tips for 2026

1. **Short-form Video** (60-90 seconds) is the most popular type of video content that now gets the most shares.

2. **Long-form Video** (3-5 minutes, and up to 10 minutes) provides more in-depth tutorials, deeper engagement and builds more authority and connection.

3. **Real Human Video** builds a stronger emotional connection, trust and engagement versus videos with graphics. Showing a person speak is much more effective for storytelling, customer testimonials and building brand authenticity.

4. **Infographic Videos** are better for explaining complex topics in a simple way. You can combine these videos with a human introduction to get a better response.

5. **Behind-the-Scenes Videos** can significantly boost audience engagement, along with building trust and transparency. These videos are especially impactful for the entertainment industry when working on a project. You can even provide fans with a virtual VIP backstage pass via video.

For 2026, the top 3 social media platforms for video engagement are *YouTube*, *Instagram* (Reels) and *TikTok*. *LinkedIn's* popularity also continues to rise for B2B and B2C videos.

YouTube Video Content also continues to surge across all generations, according to *Hootsuite.*

YouTube Video Trends for 2025, according to *Hootsuite*

YouTube remains a popular platform for users across generations.

And according to the *Pew Research Center*, "YouTube by and large is the most widely used online platform measured in our survey. Roughly eight-in-ten U.S. adults (83%) report ever using the video-based platform."

As of early 2025, Pew Research Center, also reports that approximately 35 percent of adults report regularly get news from *YouTube.*

The largest age group demographic for *YouTube's* user base is *between 25 and 34, followed by those aged 35-44, then those aged 18-24.*

Bottom line, you must be posting video content in 2026. The only question is where and how often will you post videos.

To get creative ideas, go for a walk, look at your content calendar, and film topics that connect with your audience. Ideally, you want to produce a video series with compelling stories.

Keep-it-simple by using the power of threes for your videos. Write down your three key points, and then film your insights in under two minutes.

To give you video storytelling ideas, here are some fun examples:

3 Educational Video Short Examples

5 Storytelling Techniques to Tell Insanely Good Stories
via Philipp-Humm YouTube Channel
https://www.youtube.com/shorts/mGzB9eGDV6Y
(42 seconds)

The Most Viewed YouTube Shorts
via @Jelly
https://www.youtube.com/shorts/iMHfAAyvdKM
(73 seconds)

Who is Regulating AI?
Asset Protection Attorney and Corporate Direct CEO/Founder
Garrett Sutton
via *TENERO Financial Education YouTube Channel*
https://www.youtube.com/shorts/XyGO1Rr1158
(72 seconds)

* * *

Next, let's look at entertaining videos. After attending many public relations and book marketing seminars, one of my favorite tips is **Funny = Money**.

So when you get ready to film your videos, think about ways that you can make people smile, or surprise viewers like these video examples.

3 Entertaining Video Examples

The best California dog selfies
Ellies Golden Life
via @EllieGoldenLife *YouTube Channel*
https://www.youtube.com/shorts/es5bu7C-y4Q
(62 seconds)

Chris Evans Captain America compares muscles to Thor at Comic-Con Marvel Panel
via *Goody Awards YouTube Channel*
https://www.youtube.com/watch?v=yVyFgbyue5A
(2 minutes 14 seconds, 952,000 views)

We played Shallow with amazing 9 year old Lota
Via @violin_phonix
https://www.youtube.com/shorts/PeREMRWWooo
(59 seconds, 12 Million Views)

Then, if you can combine being educational and entertaining via video, you will get an even higher engagement rate online:

3 Educational and Entertaining Video Examples

***FOX Weather*: Janet Ivey CEO Janet's Planet demonstrates 2025 Partial Solar Eclipse Viewing Tips**
>Check out her visual props!
>via *Goody PR YouTube Channel*
>https://www.youtube.com/watch?v=99fxgifMP_0
>(4 minutes 19 seconds)

***NewsNation*: How to spot Real vs. Fake Eclipse Glasses**
>*American Paper Optics* CEO John Jerit
>via *Goody PR YouTube Channel*
>https://www.youtube.com/watch?v=Zm74CxusjTg
>(3 minutes 44 seconds)

You're Wasting Your Time Creating Social Media Content
>via *Neil Patel YouTube Channel*
>https://www.youtube.com/watch?v=t9p2XbuC9Qc
>(13 minutes, 13 seconds)

* * *

Video Production and Posting Tips

To ensure your videos are seen and viewed, you will also need video production, editing and posting tips. So let's take a closer look at three tips for filming, SEO, and Playlists that can maximize your brand story's reach:

Video Filming Tips

When filming your videos, follow the tips in the Media Training Booster chapter in this book for visuals, equipment and quality. Along with wearing something that makes you look great on camera, buy a selfie light and an awesome microphone. Prepare a high-level script with three key talking points, and practice a few times before filming.

Keep in mind that authenticity is a must to connect with your audience. You do NOT want to read exactly from a script. Instead, smile, lean in, speak with conviction, and show genuine enthusiasm in your tone of voice.

For a book trailer video, an author client insisted on reading his script. To make his reading less obvious, the video includes still images with audio only.

What I recommend instead is coming up with three key points or one short story to better focus your video message, increase engagement and gain more views.

With the average attention span of an adult being only eight seconds, the most important tip that I can share is to use emphasis statements (which I just did in this sentence). You can also find more examples in the Media Training Booster chapter.

Most people stop viewing a video in the first 15 seconds if they are not interested, so you must gain their attention right away. Make your opening inviting with teasers. For example, you might say, "Keep listening to the end for a big announcement."

Be sure to select a great location for your filming. For our dating book, I filmed Great Love Reviews in the same locations where romantic comedy movies were made. Living in Los Angeles made this much easier. You don't have to go to those extremes. However, you do want to find a place with great lighting, no distractions, and where you can set up a microphone. The most important thing is you want to feel confident inside.

Post Videos with Great SEO Strategy

When you post your video on *YouTube* or any other platform, make sure that you are maximizing your SEO so that your video shows up in *Google* and/or AI search results.

As a quick summary, here are our top SEO tips for posting videos on *YouTube*. While these tips may sound obvious, most content creators put a lot of effort into their videos and rush to post them with no strategy. Please use these video SEO tips to help you reach millions of potential viewers much faster.

7 *YouTube* Video SEO Tips via *Goody PR* Blog

1. Define Long-tail Keyword Phrases for Your Video (2-3 Word Phrase).

2. Maximize Your Video Title with Keywords, Action Verbs and Numbers.

3. Write an Inviting Video Description that is at least 1 paragraph with Keywords.

4. Include 3 Video Description Hashtags using Your Keywords at the bottom of the video description.

5. Name Your Video Asset Files (video and images) with Your Keywords.

6. Post Clear, Concise and Compelling Video Content using Your Keywords.

7. Post High Quality Videos using the Best Equipment to encourage views.

This *YouTube* content-posting strategy is the secret sauce when competing for eyeballs within your industry online.

As a video SEO strategy example, our *Goody Business Book Awards* User Survey shows that *Google* Search is a top way people find this program. To support search, we regularly post *YouTube* video shorts using keyword phrases such as "top business book awards," "best business book awards" and "business book awards."

You can do this, too, for your business, book or brand. Think about your keywords, and then apply these seven Video SEO Tips.

Video Playlist Tips

In addition to filming high quality video and posting with an SEO strategy, you can increase search results by posting your videos on *YouTube Playlists*.

This Playlist approach works great if you already have a lot of Subscribers on your *YouTube Channel*. So instead of setting up a new channel, create a Playlist to organize videos connected to a common theme or topic.

You can also write a title and short description for each Playlist, so that it shows up in search results.

As an example, I started using a *YouTube* Playlist approach for different *Goody PR* services, projects and clients versus creating a new *YouTube Channel*. It really helped showcase our 477+ videos by curating them based on the topic. To give you ideas for how to organize your videos, here are five *Goody PR* YouTube Channel Playlists:

1. Top Media Examples for *Goody PR* agency clients

2. *Goody PR*: Client Media Interviews

3. *Goody PR*: *American Paper Optics* Eclipse Glasses

4. *Goody Business Book Awards*

5. *8-Second Branding* Podcast

> **Video Playlist Example: *APO/* Eclipse Glasses Publicity Campaign**
>
> ***Goody PR* YouTube Channel Playlist features 55 Videos**

A *YouTube Playlist* can provide you with an easy way to create a library of your content by subject area and shows up in search results. Let's look at an example.

To make it easy for our VIP client, *American Paper Optics/ Eclipse Glasses*, I created a custom Playlist on our *Goody PR YouTube Channel* featuring their media interviews. This Playlist has a separate link to a page that highlights their work only and can be easily shared online.

This custom Playlist includes 55 videos with top TV, print, radio and podcast interviews, along with *Video Shorts* created to magnify their stories.

Media Interview Video Examples:

- ***Scripps News***: Why *American Paper Optics* CEO John Jerit built Eclipse Glasses and 3D Eyewear Business
- ***CBS Saturday Morning***: How *American Paper Optics* made 75 Million Eclipse Glasses for April 8 2024

- ***FOX Weather***: How *American Paper Optics* made *NASA* Eclipse Glasses for 2023 and 2024 Eclipses

YouTube Shorts Examples:

- Totality Over Texas —Clouds Break for Magic Total Solar Eclipse April 8 2024

- 3 Easy Steps —How to use *Solar Snap The Eclipse App* for Epic Photos of April 8 Total Solar Eclipse

- *People Magazine* features *American Paper Optics* CEO John Jerit and Eclipse Glasses Safety Tips

- *The Moonies* Author Meg Jerit interviews Dog Nipsey about her New Total Solar Eclipse Book

- How to get Free *Warby Parker* Eclipse Glasses for April 8 Total Solar Eclipse

6.3 Use AI to Maximize Digital Marketing and PR Efficiencies

As we wrap-up this Digital Marketing Booster chapter, it's hard to avoid mentioning AI as a way to make your social media and publicity campaigns more efficient. This area is relatively new to online promotions and public relations, and will continue to evolve.

While many believe AI is still in a "Pilot Phase" for marketing, you want to embrace it as a content creator and communications professional. AI is here, and is about to influence every area of our daily lives.

Based on our research and use of AI, here are the top eight trends that you should consider when creating and posting your digital marketing content:

8 AI Content Creator Tips for 2026

1. Use AI to improve your social media process and efficiencies.

2. Use AI to automate content distribution to save time.

3. Use AI to research your industry trends and resources.

4. Use AI to help you develop creative ideas and graphics.

5. To maintain trust, be transparent about when you use AI.

6. Fact check and verify any AI content with credible sources.

7. Use AI to better understand your audience and results.

8. Always make human connections a top priority over AI.

Warning: Humans versus AI

While there are many benefits for marketers using AI, I want to start with a warning. You must always maintain your authenticity online as a human being first. So think strategically every step of the way as you dive into the age of AI.

For the best digital marketing results, always share genuine content using personal storytelling, empathy and feelings to connect emotionally with fans.

Remember, people want to follow people and companies that they like and trust online. If you start posting too much AI content, your audience is going to be turned off because they want to see a real person.

Proceed with Care and Monitoring in the Age of AI

As a small business owner, thought leader or brand, your credibility can be lost with one post made by AI. While a fun video with cool graphics generated by AI can be very entertaining, always credit the AI tools used. Otherwise, you might lose the trust of your audience.

You also want to monitor people posting content about you that is a deepfake. This content may show a person's likeness, voice or expressions doing something that they did not really do. Misleading deepfakes have negatively depicted many public figures, including Elon Musk, Taylor Swift and Oprah Winfrey.

I've also seen several cases where Podcast Hosts generated AI images of our clients for their show promotions. While the hosts had best intentions in mind, the photos were so distorted that they looked fake. To protect their personal brands, the spokespeople requested that these AI images be replaced with their actual headshot photos.

Write Your Own Content vs. AI to Maintain Authenticity

While no one is policing social media for AI posts, your followers and customers want unpolished content that is the real deal. Fans want genuine, transparent and consistent content to foster long-term loyalty and trust.

It's very important that you continue to write your own content in the age of AI. Some colleagues challenge me by saying, "Oh Liz, I wrote the draft, but then I had AI edit it." In my opinion, the work is no longer your original content if AI changed it.

And please don't steal content from others or AI without giving full credit. When I taught Digital Marketing at *UCLA Extension* for seven years, Instructors were given a tool to check to see if anyone was using someone else's work. In one case, I was shocked (maybe you are not) that someone took an entire *Inc. Magazine* story and submitted it as their own essay for an assignment.

The primary penalty that the school asked me to give the student was a 0 on the assignment. They were also given a warning that if they used someone else's work again without giving credit, they MIGHT face disciplinary action.

With AI content exploding, we are also seeing publishers take extra precautions.

AI Content Check Examples: Psychology Today and Amazon

For example, a *Psychology Today* Editor informed me that their team is now using AI tools to check Contributor articles before approving them for publication. Fortunately, *Goody PR* recently secured two national columns/blogs for clients in this national publication. I shared this update with these doctor/author clients.

In another example, one of our clients submitted a new book to *Amazon* that was a companion journal for their previous book.

While the author wrote their new journal questions, *Amazon* questioned whether the book was written by AI. After confirming that she wrote it, *Amazon* finally agreed to publish the book.

Expect more publishers to do these extra AI checks in 2026 and beyond.

While it can take more time to write your own words, you must protect your brand voice and integrity online. So seriously, don't use AI to write or edit your books, articles or columns. You can use AI to do research and generate ideas. However, avoid publishing an article using AI content with your name on it as the author.

AI Regulation is the "Wild, Wild West" Now

As a small business owner, you are now facing mixed messages with AI. *Corporate Direct* CEO/Founder, Asset Protection Attorney and Award-Winning Author Garrett Z. Sutton calls AI regulation the "Wild-Wild West" because it has been left to the states with no central guidelines from the federal government as of December 2025.

This AI regulation by the states has several impacts. For example, if you run a business in multiple states (Utah and California, for example), and they have different AI laws, then you have to meet the requirements in both states.

Focus on Improving Digital Marketing and PR Efficiencies with AI

To maximize your marketing with AI, look for ways to improve your operations and efficiencies. You can use AI tools to evaluate your digital marketing and publicity workflows. Let it help you find ways to lower costs and improve results.

To fast-track your digital marketing results, schedule regular brainstorming meetings with your team. Identify ways to use AI in smart ways using new tools.

For example, you can use AI tools to research what type of content will increase your engagement rate the most.

In addition, using the right social media management tools can save you both time and money. You can strategically schedule posts based on your content calendar to connect with your audience in a timely way. AI can also produce invaluable reports.

Email marketing tools are another way to send custom pitches to reporters efficiently. *Goody PR* uses tools to personalize emails, and track results. For example, you can write a customized subject line with their outlet name, along with including their first name and outlet in the body of your email.

Use AI Tools to enhance your Digital Marketing Toolkit

You can use AI tools to improve your digital marketing toolkit for a brand, business or book. Let's take a closer look at one of our favorite AI tools.

- *Rev.com* **AI Transcripts**: For media and video transcripts, one of our favorite tools to use is *Rev.com*. While *YouTube* has video transcripts now available, Rev.com can provide you with a transcript generated by AI in a very short timeframe in a Word doc and/or PDF. You can then use these transcripts to pull soundbites, draft pitches, and/or use a basis for a story submission.

- *NotebookLM* **AI Tools** - In addition, one of our favorite AI tools is *NotebookLM* for many reasons. These tools are especially helpful for anyone with a book or brand to promote.

AI Resource Example: *NotebookLM* Tools

As a CEO, marketer or author, you may want to try *NotebookLM* to generate audio summaries, study outlines and even infographics.

For our *8-Second PR* book, I generated a 20-minute audio summary of the book. We ran it through the tool a few times because some of the information was not accurate at first. As you know, AI does not get everything right. After generating the audio summary three times, *NotebookLM* produced a comprehensive audio summary that was both positive and accurate.

As a result, I created a custom video using this audio and custom graphics. This video was then posted on our *Goody PR YouTube* Channel using our SEO keywords to maximize reach. Because *8-Second PR* does not have an audiobook, this summary was a quick and easy solution.

NotebookLM recently launched an Infographic Generator tool. You can generate an infographic based on a book, document or video. As a result, I entered a *YouTube* link to our *Goody PR Overview* video that explains how we help small businesses and authors get earned media coverage.

As a result, *NotebookLM* created the infographic below that features our 3-step process. And to multi-purpose this content, I shared it on social media on *Facebook* and *LinkedIn* to showcase our work for potential clients. You can do this too.

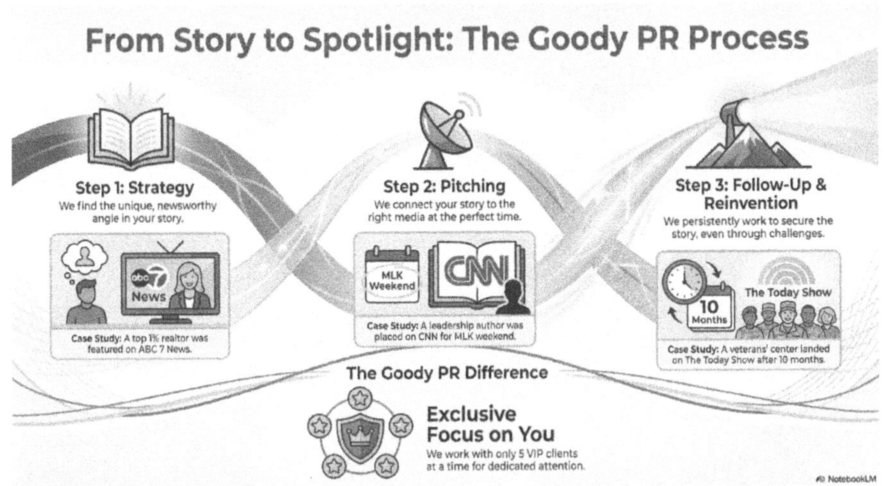

Use AI to Predict Behavior

According to *McKinsey*, almost 88 percent of organizations they surveyed are now using AI in some format. In another *McKinsey* report, they emphasize that time spent online is not as important as getting someone's attention.

As a reminder, marketers should use AI to tell better stories that emotionally connect with your target audience. In addition, AI can help you predict what your audience will do next after engaging with your content.

SOURCE
McKinsey: The State of AI in 2025 (November 5, 2025)

There are endless uses of AI for marketers. And as I mentioned, we are in the early stage of the Age of AI. In addition to *NotebookLM*, consider ten other AI marketing tools listed below as bonus content from a video marketing and AI expert.

> **Bonus Content: 10 Other AI Marketing Tools**
>
> **By Austin Armstrong, CEO *Syllaby***

You can use these top 10 AI tools to enhance your digital marketing efforts. This summary was posted by Austin Armstrong, CEO of *Syllaby* and Co-Founder of *AI Marketing World Conference*, on *LinkedIn*. Armstrong is a recognized speaker at many digital marketing conferences. He often posts top 10 lists that are very helpful.

1. *ChaptGPT* —solves anything
2. *Syllaby.io* —saves 70 percent of your time and budget for video production and video ads
3. Ranked.ai —rank your website in AI
4. Heygen.com —creates AI avatars
5. Soundraw.io —produces music in seconds
6. Gemini.google.com —Nano Banana Pro. Generate images
7. Submagic.com —turn long videos into shorts
8. SlidesAI.io —makes presentations for you
9. PicWish.com —edits photos faster
10. Fastread.io —creates eBooks

ABOUT: Austin Armstrong is the author of the book *VIRALITY!*, a keynote speaker, 2X 7-figure entrepreneur, host of the podcast

BusinessTok, and CEO of *Syllaby*, an AI startup that helps content creators create, schedule, and publish videos in minutes.

As you wrap-up this Digital Marketing Booster chapter, let's review your Action Items and next steps. There is a lot of content in this chapter. Take time to absorb it all, and then map out your digital marketing strategy.

STEP 6:
Your Digital Marketing Booster Action Items Recap

To reach millions of potential customers faster, here are your 3 Digital Marketing Booster Action Items Recap to enhance your social media, video and AI.

6.1 Define Your Digital Marketing Strategy with Top 3 Platforms.

Document your big picture Digital Marketing Strategy that includes your goals and top 3 platforms. Define your ideal target audience, and focus your energies on where they consume their online content.

6.2 Produce Video Storytelling Content that Educates and Entertains.

Identify 3 video storytelling ideas as a series. Define three key topics for each video that can entertain and educate your audience. Schedule the filming and editing on your calendar for these videos.

6.3 Use AI to Maximize Digital Marketing and PR Efficiencies.

Identify three ways to improve your overall marketing workflows using AI, all while maintaining authentic human connections and integrity online.

You now have the Digital Marketing Booster tools and tips to build a comprehensive strategy to skyrocket your brand to the next level. With the right plan and human-focused content, millions of fans will FALL IN LOVE with your company, product or book.

In the next chapter, **Step 7: Book Marketing Booster**, you will learn more about how to extend your reach by thinking about marketing Before, During and After launching a book or product. And then, we will wrap up with the final chapter, **Step 8: Top Media Booster** that features how to make your story go viral.

BOOK MARKETING BOOSTER:
Attract Media Before, During and After Publishing

Ventura Highway in the sunshine.

–Ventura Highway by America

Do you know that you should ALWAYS start thinking about marketing from the minute that you decide to write a book? And did you know that the bulk of your marketing preparation should happen BEFORE you publish your book? Once you make the bold decision to write a book, you need to start mapping out your book marketing plan.

Our goal is to make your author journey easier so that you feel more sunshine versus frustration. As the song says, you are about to merge onto a *Ventura Highway*, so buckle up.

This comprehensive Book Marketing Booster checklist is based on decades of experience as both a published author and top book publicist, promoting primarily nonfiction books. You will find a comprehensive summary with action items for three publishing phases: Before, During and After launch.

To help you have a positive experience as an author, attract earned media coverage, and ultimately generate revenue from your book, you must think like a marketer during every step of the process described in this chapter.

IMPORTANT READER NOTE

If you are not an aspiring author, author and/or book publicist, you may decide to skip this chapter.

However, If you ever thought of launching a business or product, these marketing steps may be helpful. It's your choice.

Just as working towards a major life goal, writing and publishing a book is an uphill trek. You can learn practical tips with specific action items to attract more media.

Yes, it can be an overwhelming undertaking to publish a book. However, it's also one of the most rewarding things you can do in life. Don't give up on your dream to be a published author. You can do this!

If you follow this Book Marketing Booster Checklist with 75 action items, you are much more likely to be in the top 4 percent of authors who sell 1,000+ books.

There will also be things in this checklist that you may want to skip, but take the time to review it carefully. People tell me all the time that they want to write a book, but they have no idea what is involved.

If you're truly serious about writing and promoting a book (or product), these steps can help you navigate the process successfully and avoid costly mistakes.

STEP 7: Book Marketing Boosters

7.1 Phase 1: Develop Pre-Launch Book Marketing Strategy
(Action Items 1-45)

7.2 Phase 2: Implement Book Launch Month Promotions
(Action Items 46-58)

7.3 Phase 3: Plan Post-Launch Campaigns for Long-Term Success
(Action Items 59-75)

Keep in mind that promoting a book is an even bigger job than writing it.

If you follow these marketing steps from the beginning, it will be much easier when you are finally ready to launch.

Many authors fantasize about a planned national book tour after watching *Hallmark Channel* movies about authors. It's a nice dream, but it rarely happens that way, unless you are a celebrity. Instead, you must start your book marketing planning way before a launch, and do the hard work to build momentum.

Most authors do not know:

Over 90 percent of books sell fewer than 1,000 copies; 50 percent of books sell fewer than 12 copies.

According to Slate

These low book sales numbers are likely the result of many factors, which may include competitive books, lack of uniqueness and/or little to no marketing budget and planning.

So are you ready to roll up your sleeves and get creative by thinking like a Book Marketer from the beginning? The world wants to hear your personal story and advice tips, but winning hearts and minds is an art that takes time, resources, and investment.

I've lost count of how many authors I've met who skipped some of these book marketing steps. As a result, I've coached many authors on how to revise and re-launch their personal brand, book messaging, and websites.

If you want to be in the Top 10 percent of authors, keep reading about these three Book Marketing Booster phases and action items. Take notes, and come back to this chapter.

7.1 Phase 1:Develop Pre-Launch Book Marketing Strategy

Your Pre-Launch Book Marketing Strategy Phase is probably the most important because it sets the stage for success. During this Phase 1, you must clearly define the uniqueness of your book and/ or product, outline the core benefits for readers, and develop a book launch strategy.

To emphasize why pre-launch planning is so important, here are three author PR examples. Each of these authors short-changed this process and called *Goody PR* at the last minute in a panic. Instead, you want to be always thinking ahead.

3 Author Publicity Planning Examples

- **Example 1: Hired PR Agency 3 Weeks Before Book Launch** —For the book *Hustle, Flow or Let it Go?* by Public Health Professor and 2 times TEDx Speaker Dr. Portia Preston, the author met with us initially in April 2025. After our initial call, her response was that the publisher would take care of all of her publicity. Fast-forward to 3 months later, and I get a panic text on a Sunday in July that said, "Are you still available? I need to hire you tomorrow for my book launch in three weeks." She signed a contract three days later.

- **Example 2: Hired PR Agency on Book Launch Day** —In a second case, I was hired by Author and Producer Rob Schwartz, who literally signed our PR contract on the publication day of his book *The Wisdom of Morrie*. Rob wrote the Foreword for this self-help book that was written by his late father, Morrie Schwartz. His father was the subject of the blockbuster book *Tuesdays with Morrie*. It was posthumously published, and Rob wanted to put extra PR efforts on the book. By working closely with Rob and his publisher, I got a launch press release out within 48 hours. As context, most publicists take the first month to get ready for a book launch, so this was at warp speed!

- **Example 3: Hired PR Agency 2 Months After Book Launch** —In a third case, I was hired two months after the WWII book *40 Thieves on Saipan* was published. Co-Authors Joseph Tachovsky and Cynthia Kraack realized that their publisher was no longer promoting their work, and wanted help. Fortunately, *40 Thieves on Saipan* was really well-written with a powerful backstory. We found many publicity opportunities for it that are described throughout this book.

In all three of these examples, the authors put so much work into their writing projects —and yet they skipped important Book Marketing Boosters described here for you.

Let's review the Book Marketing Boosters for your Phase 1 Pre-Launch Phase, which involves over 60 percent of the overall action items.

Phase 1 - Book Marketing Boosters —Before Launch

To make it easier for you, Phase 1 is broken up into these 7 sub-sections:

Phase 1.1 — Publicity Big Picture Plan
Phase 1.2 — Select Your Book Title Carefully
Phase 1.3 — Write Your Book with Marketing in Mind
Phase 1.4 — Create a Professional Looking Book
Phase 1.5 — Create a Digital Marketing Strategy
Phase 1.6 — Develop a Book Publicity Launch Strategy
Phase 1.7 — Develop an Amazon Book Marketing Plan

Phase 1.1 — Publicity Big Picture Plan

From the first day that you start writing, you want to find creative ways to position your book/product/story by adding sex appeal or story magic. The last thing that you want your book to be is boring. So think about unique stories that can entertain and educate your audience—and attract media coverage.

1. Draft Book Marketing Success Plan —At least six months before launch, start drafting your **book marketing plan** and/or hire a PR agency who has promoted authors. Use these Book Marketing Boosters as your master project plan template. I've already created an Excel file template with these steps for several author clients to track their progress. You can do this, too.

2. Define Marketing Budget —Develop a **Marketing and PR Budget** for your new book and work with a book marketing expert(s). You worked really hard on your book, so make sure you have money, time and resources ready to promote it.

When asked about the amount you need for a book marketing budget, I'd say the range is $20k - $100k. Even if you have all the time in the world to do-it-yourself, you really want to hire professionals who have specific skillsets that are not your strengths.

Phase 1.2 — Select Your Book Title Carefully

3. Select Unique Title and Sub-Title —Before you go too far in your writing process, make sure that you select a **unique book title that is 3-5 words and a unique sub-title that is 3-7 words.**

You also must avoid picking an over-used cliché title such as *One-Hit Wonder, The Closer* or *Playing for Keeps*. It is much harder to promote a unique and memorable website when so many other books have the same title. Do your research on *Google, Amazon,* and *GoDaddy* to find out if anyone has your title, and choose wisely.

If there are other books with the same title, our recommendation is to choose a different one.

4. Find Titles that Boost Your Book SEO/AI Search Results — Select a book title that includes keywords and phrases to boost your SEO(Search Engine Optimization) and AI search results. Amazon is a top search engine. So if your book is about how to be a successful entrepreneur, put those word in your title and/or sub-title.

5. Buy Your BookTitle.com URL —Always buy your exact book title URL on GoDaddy. If you cannot get an exact match website for the dot com, pick another book title. And even if you already have a website, buy your BookTitle.com anyway so you can forward it to your main website. You can also buy your TitleBook.com.

Phase 1.3 — Write Your Book with Marketing in Mind

6. Go to a Writer's Conference or Get Professional Help — If you've never written a book, it's always a good idea to go to a writers' conference, book marketing seminar and/or hire a professional to help you get on a success path.

7. Define Book Uniqueness —You must define how your book is different from every other book like it. For example, my dating book, *Smart Man Hunting: A Fast-Track Guide to Finding Mr. Right*, was unique because it included 26 Man Codes (*All Sports Fanatic, Bachelor Available, Confident Metro Male*) for the different personality types.

Our man codes were organized from A-Z as a compatibility guide for couples. I made up these light-hearted codes at parties in Los Angeles to bring some levity to the dating scene. Each code had a real-life and movie example. It was a fun and new way to talk about dating. This unique content helped me secure the majority of my 500+ media hits.

8. Share Your Personal Backstory —You always want to explain **Your WHY** in a Preface or Introduction to connect with your readers. Your backstory is the story magic behind your book that can attract media coverage. For example, I recommended that Author Rich Fettke share his backstory in the Preface for his book, *The Wise Investor*. Both Rich and his main character changed careers and became real estate investors. In Rich's case, he changed careers after surviving cancer. After his book was published, Rich told me that this life-changing moment was the top topic reporters wanted to discuss.

9. Define Reader Benefits —In your Introduction and/or back cover, clearly identify the top 3-5 reasons someone should read your book. You also want to explain who is your target audience, and how your book can help them. By being upfront, you can attract the right readers. If you've skipped this step, go back and add it, and then publish an updated book version —it's that important.

10. Write for Your Audience —Remember, your book and media pitches CANNOT be ALL about you! Don't bore your readers! Instead, you want to use words that speak to your readers. **Include these two magic words: You and Your.** Otherwise, it may be viewed as a "vanity project" by reporters. Speaking to your audience will boost sales.

11. Add Feelings —Emotionally connect with your audience by describing feelings throughout your book. We are beyond grateful to you for reading this book, and genuinely want you to succeed.

12. Include Tips Throughout —To sell more books, always include helpful TIPS that can improve the lives of your target audience. Reporters also want you to "entertain and/or educate" their audience, so write a book that does both. And add short summaries with key takeaways at the end of each chapter, even if it's a memoir.

13. Provide Specific Examples —Include specific examples related to your topic. People LOVE connecting with personal stories versus just-the-facts. So dig deep, and add meaningful stories to get your points across in a memorable way.

14. Get Book Testimonials —Ask for book endorsements from experts to add more credibility. These book blurbs can go on your *Amazon* page, back cover, and/or inside the book to give it more credibility. Think about 10-20 key influencers in your book genre and/or industry. Ask them if they can write a blurb for your book, and then send them a short summary to provide context. You may also want to send the Table of Contents and/or the book draft as a PDF. Give them a deadline, and follow-up.

For my dating book, I was really fortunate to get an endorsement from John Gray PhD (Author, *Men are from Mars, Women are from Venus*). He wrote the recommendation himself, after six months of follow-up. For my PR books, I asked journalists, mentors and clients for endorsements.

15. Ask for Client Testimonials —If you have clients, ask them for testimonials for the back of your book and/or post on your website. These testimonials establish you as an industry thought leader, and add credibility to your book and business.

16. Write Short and Long Author Bios —You must write both short and long bios about yourself for your book and media interviews. You want a powerful short bio for the back cover with your name, title, company, accomplishments, awards and top media. You also want a one-page author bio for inside the back of your book. Include a headshot photo, your backstory, fun facts, main website(s), social media handles, and hashtags.

17. Define Multiple Streams of Income —Despite what you see in the movies, you cannot live on book royalites alone. You must have multiple streams of income! So you always want to include cross-promotions throughout your book and/or at the end about your OTHER products and services. I always tell authors that your book royalties will not pay our retainer fee. Instead, you want your book to be a LEAD GENERATOR that directs people to buy a bigger-ticket item from you.

For example, when I did PR for Tom Wheelwright, CEO of *WealthAbility*, the number one source of new clients for his tax-strategy business was people who read his *Tax-Free Wealth* book. Tom's consistent media coverage resulted in book sales that led to clients. It was a perfect business and publicity match, which is probably why he hired *Goody PR* for 5+ years.

Many book marketing experts advised me over the years that "Your book is just a business card in the door."

To illustrate how authors can generate multiple streams of income with a book, below is an infographic that I created using *NotebookLM* based on a *Goody PR* video. This infographic is called 3 PRO PUBLICIST TIPS FOR NON-FICTION AUTHORS.

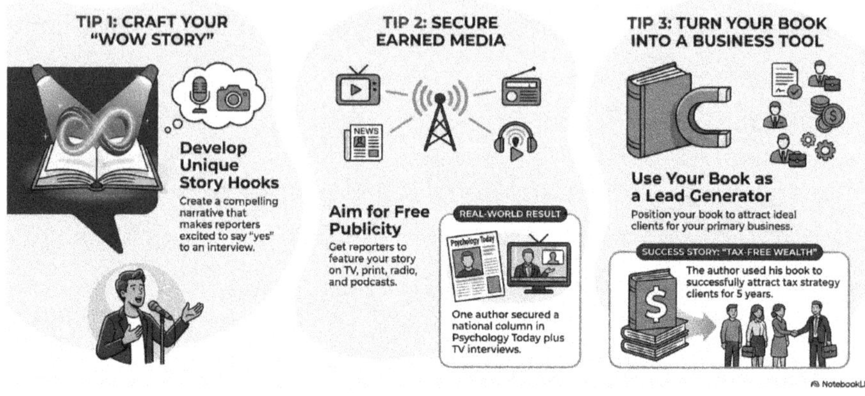

Phase 1.4 — Create a Professional Looking Book

18. Define Publisher and Get Help —In addition to writing a great book, you need to determine WHO will publish your book. You may want to self-publish, use a hybrid publisher, and/or find a literary agent and a traditional publisher. You have MANY options as an author. To make the best decision, you can research on your own, ask other authors for advice, and/or get help from some of the top book publishing coaches.

To help you, below are book publishing pros to consider hiring.

4 Top Book Publishing Pros whom I recommend:

1. **Randy Peyser at AuthorOneStop.com** is our go-to recommendation for authors who want a book deal with a top 5 publisher. Randy is a master at writing book proposals and pitching books, and has a team of ghostwriters. She has solid connections with literary agents and publishers, and secured 16 book deals last year alone with top publishers, including *Wiley, Simon & Schuster,* and *Hay House*. Randy can also help you turn your book into a screenplay.

2. **Liz Dubelman at VidLit Productions** (vidlit.com) is a passionate publishing consultant, content creator, and book marketer. Liz can guide you through

the entire publishing process and brings creative, strategic marketing ideas tailored to each author's goals. She specializes in Substack newsletter growth, and can manage your book submissions to *Ingram* and *Amazon*. I've worked with Liz on several author campaigns and highly recommend her.

3. **Debra Eckerling at TheBookProposalExpert.com** can help you write a solid book proposal and/or book. She can also help you find a literary agent or publisher. You must include a Book Marketing Plan in your book proposal, so everything in this chapter can help you with that section.

4. **Ruth Klein** (https://ruthklein.com/) writes winning book proposals for book deals with traditional publishers and helps craft speeches for paid speaking opportunities. Reach out to her to become a guest on her TV show, *The Book Club with Ruth Klein*…reaching an audience of millions.

19. Buy Book Serial Numbers —If you have a publisher, they will do this book registration step for you. If you are self-publishing, you must buy an **ISBN** (International Standard Book Number). It is a unique 13-digit identifier, which is the serial number for each book version. You can buy ISBNs online from *Bowker*. You need separate ISBNs for your hardback, paperback and eBook versions. You also want to purchase a 10-digit **ASIN** (Amazon Standard Identification Number) for your audiobook for *Amazon*. You can buy these numbers individually, or get a package with a discount.

20. Hire a Book Editor —Always hire a professional book editor, because you need someone else to review your work. There are several types of book editors. The two main types include 1. Developmental and Structural Editor (big picture strategy, plot and pace) and 2. Copy Editor (corrects grammar, typos and ensures consistency).

I proofread my *8-Second PR* book for the tenth time at 3 AM, and that's not the best plan ☺. I highly recommend that you hire professionals to help you. You can also go to Reedsy.com to hire a contractor or ask a friend for a book editor referral.

21. Hire an Internal Book Designer —After you have completely finished editing your book, it's time to do the internal book design.

If you have a publisher, they will do this step. If you are self-publishing, you must hire a professional interior book designer. Most designers will charge you an hourly rate. And don't turn your book over to them until you are really ready. If you want to make more edits, get ready to pay the designer more. Once they start formatting your book, you can no longer make edits on your own.

The internal book designer creates a print-ready book based on different templates for your hardback, paperback, and eBook. Determine the size of your book first (6x9 inches for this book), and then download the templates from *Amazon* and *Ingram*.

If this step is not done correctly, your book will be rejected by *Ingram* and *Amazon* when it is submitted for publication.

As an example, my *8-Second PR* book was rejected by *Amazon* at first because both the book cover and internal design were off by 1/8 inch. This issue delayed the book launch by a few days because each designer had to make updates. Please, don't even try to do the internal book design on your own.

22. Hire a Book Cover Designer —You also want to hire a professional book cover designer, unless you have a publisher who is paying a graphic artist. To develop the best book cover, give the graphic artist direction on your vision. Once you have a few drafts, ask for honest feedback from friends, along with people you don't know. Your book cover image is the first thing any potential reader sees, so it must be awesome!

For the final edition of my dating book, *Kensington Books Publishing* chose the cover without consulting me. This approach is typical for a publisher because they invest a lot in your book marketing. I did not like the cover, but they did not want author feedback.

If you self-publish, you can hire the designer and have complete control over approvals. For my *8-Second PR: New Public Relations Crash Course* (2022) book, I researched and found a fantastic book cover designer, Heidi North. We went back and forth probably 10 times until we got the final cover design, and it really sells the book.

23. Get Professional Author Photos —To support your thought leader brand, hire a professional photographer to take your headshot photos. These photos are very important for your back cover, author photo inside the book, and media interviews. While iPhones take great photos today, it is always best to get professional photos. You want great lighting, hair, makeup, colors, props, and expressions. For my books and author clients, I've hired the same professional photographer in Los Angeles. For the best professional headshots, I highly recommend **Bader Howar Photography**. Her work is a gamechanger for authors, actors and brands.

24. **Get help with Audiobook** —While many authors record their audiobook using platforms such as *Audible* (owned by *Amazon)*, consider hiring production experts. Creating an audiobook is not as easy as it looks. Investing in production services will make your audiobook quality much better, and ultimately increase sales.

You can also hire an actor, narrator or voiceover artist to record your audiobook in a studio. For example, for *The Wisdom of Morrie*, *Blackstone Publishing* hired Actor Steven Weber (best known for *Wings* and *Curb Your Enthusiasm*). You also can include multiple voices and personalities in your audiobook.

Phase 1.5 — Create a Digital Marketing Strategy

25. Create a Digital Marketing Strategy —You can go back to Step 6: Digital Marketing Booster chapter to get creative ideas. If you're writing a book proposal, agents and publishers will want to see your digital marketing plan. Select your top 3 platforms, develop a digital marketing strategy and post based on a content calendar.

26. Embrace Social Media Marketing —You must be passionate about your social media marketing as an author. It's one of the best ways to build a fan base and get people engaged with your brand. You can do it yourself and/or hire social media professionals. While the majority of authors think a DIY (do-it-yourself) approach is best, it's a very time consuming commitment.

To provide perspective on the importance, *AuthorOneStop* Founder Randy Peyser tells authors they need a minimum of 30,000 followers to attract a top 5 publisher deal.

27. Launch a Book Website or Custom Page —To make it really easy to find your book online, develop an engaging book website.

This book marketing step is non-negotiable. If you buy your BookTitle.com URL, you also can forward it to a custom page on your company website. Include a book summary, top reviews and endorsements with SEO keywords in both scenarios.

28. Create a Book Trailer Video —To connect emotionally with a broader audience, hire a professional and/or film a short book trailer video that is a maximum of two minutes. Share this video on your website, social media, and in a book-launch press release. This book trailer does not have to be a huge effort. However, it is a very important way to connect emotionally with your audience via video. Talk about your personal WHY, the backstory, and how your book can help readers.

29. Add Social Media Handles to Your Book Bio —Your ABOUT THE AUTHOR page should include your social media handles and hashtags in the back of the book. You want to make it really EASY for people to find and follow you online.

30. Create Your Digital Press Kit —Work with your public relations and marketing teams to create a Digital Press Kit that we discussed previously. To help reporters share your story, include a book summary, short bio, Q and A, and potential visuals.

31. Prepare a Social Media Ad Budget —Because so many social media platforms now want you to "pay to play," create a digital marketing budget. Ads will let you boost your videos and reach your target market faster.

Phase 1.6 — Develop a Book Publicity Launch Strategy

32. Plan Your Book Publicity Approach —Consider hiring a PR firm prior to your book launch. Based on your input, they can develop a book marketing strategy, and start scheduling pre-launch interviews.

Based on case studies mentioned previously, *Goody PR* has been hired by many nonfiction authors before, during and after a book launch. However, your best approach is to hire a PR team at least 3-6 months before your publication date.

33. Secure Niche Podcast Interviews Pre-Launch —Focus your pre-launch book PR phase on scheduling niche podcast and print interviews based on your subject area. This approach can produce a library of content published in support of your launch.

> **Media Example: Author Pre-Launch Podcast Interview Strategy**
>
> **30+ Podcasts for *Raising Good Humans Every Day* Author**

When *Raising Good Humans* Author Hunter Clarke-Fields first called me, I was excited there was time to do pre-book launch PR for her sequel, *Raising Good Humans Every Day: 50 Simple Ways to Press Pause, Stay Present and Connect with Your Kids*. Hunter's goal was to be on top parenting podcasts to reach her ideal target audience, which was mostly moms.

As a result, our team researched the top parenting podcasts in this niche, started pitching and scheduled interviews. In the pitch emails, I asked the hosts if they could wait to publish their interview in sync with the book launch date.

As a result of this strategy, *Goody PR* secured 30+ parenting podcast interviews by working closely with Hunter. And about half of these pre-launch book interviews were then published around the same time as her book launch date.

In addition to this podcast blitz campaign, our team worked closely with Hunter's publisher during the pre-launch phase. Most publishers promote right before a launch, and then pull back because they move on to the next book. As a result, publishers are happy to work with an external PR agency who can maintain the publicity momentum.

Overall, a pre-launch podcast strategy is the reason many authors hire *Goody PR* or other PR firms during this Phase 1: Pre-Launch Book Marketing phase. Your public relations program should ramp up during Phase 2: Book Launch Month Promotions and expand with new ideas during Phase 3: Post Launch for Long-Term Publicity.

34. Seek Book Reviews —Submit your book for reviews prior to launch using a PDF or Advanced Reader Copy (ARC). In an ideal world, several book reviewers will read your book and write a free review. While I don't recommend paying for media coverage, there are exceptions. Authors can pay for a professional book review from *BookLife* (part of *Publisher's Weekly*) or *Kirkus Reviews*, and/ or use the *NetGalley* platform.

35. Create a Pre-Sale Press Release —Ask you PR team to send out a book pre-sales press release announcement as soon as your book is available for pre-sale on *Amazon*. If you self-publish on *Amazon*, they will limit your pre-sales to eBooks only, which is fine.

36. Do a Book Cover Reveal —As part of your pre-launch campaign, do a Book Cover Reveal countdown on social media to build buzz and excitement. Don't just post your book cover or casually share it publicly. Your book cover is a major part of your marketing, so make it a big deal.

37. Build Book Buzz with Launch Countdown —You can build extra excitement for your book with a launch countdown campaign on social media and/or your website(s). Add a countdown clock widget to your website, post countdown videos and/or graphics on social media, and/or do a sweepstakes contest. You can do book giveaways and offer other prizes —as long as you do not ask for a book review in return.

38. Secure Bookstore Talks —Pitch and schedule potential book talk and signing events at bookstores, schools, libraries, corporations and other related venues. To maximize these opportunities, pitch your event months in advance. Your publicist may or may not offer these services. Honestly, you will not have a lot of book sales at a bookstore event (10-20 is a best guess), but it can result in great publicity.

Author Book Talk and Publicity Example:

Barnes and Noble Santa Monica Book Talk for Dr. Laura Gabayan

Book talks do not just magically happen, so you need to plan way ahead. The events managers usually schedule authors months in advance, so start reaching out to them during your pre-launch phase.

After many failed attempts via email and phone, it took physically walking into *Barnes and Noble Santa Monica* several times to meet the events manager and secure a book talk for Dr. Laura Gabayan, Author of *Common Wisdom*. This book talk was scheduled two months later for a Saturday afternoon in July.

To promote this event, I set up a paid ad campaign in the local *Patch* online that included a short description, author and book photo, and links to this event.

In addition, I was able to secure a feature story in the local *Santa Monica Daily Press* print and online editions the week of the event. To get this coverage, I wrote the story draft, submitted it to the editor with a photo, and then called as a follow-up 3 times.

In addition, our *Goody PR* team submitted this book talk event to calendars for five other local publications.

The good news is that Dr. Laura Gabayan's book talk drew full-capacity attendance. Many people showed up with the local newspaper story in their hands. While events can be difficult to get people to attend, local publicity really can help.

In addition, make sure that you take a good camera and videographer to all live events so you can build a library of action photos showing you as speaker.

This book talk event was later covered by *The Jewish Journal* with a write-up and photo in their weekly *Movers and Shakers* column. For this recap, I also wrote a draft to make it easier for the reporter to cover it within a timely manner.

To magnify your story, you always want to multi-purpose your book talks.

39. Secure Corporate Speaking Events —In addition to scheduling bookstore talks, you want to secure speaker opportunities at conferences, corporations and local clubs. If you have a huge following online, title, brand and/or book, you may be fortunate to secure a paid speaking engagement. If you get this lucky, ask the host if they want to buy a bulk order of books as part of your negotiated contract. Alternatively, ask for permission to sell books at the back of the room after your talk.

As an example, one of our clients secured a paid speaking gig at a major company. During her negotiations, the company agreed to buy hundreds of book copies for this talk. Her advice is to ask questions about how a bulk book purchase may impact your speaker's fee. In this case, the author was ok with her fee being reduced if the corporation bought a lot of books. Review the details in your speaker contract, and negotiate in writing to avoid any misunderstandings.

Phase 1.7 — Develop an Amazon Book Marketing Plan

Because *Amazon* is ranked as the largest e-commerce search engine in the world, you cannot afford to skip an *Amazon* ad campaign for your book. *Amazon* is often considered the second or third largest search engine. In many ways, it works like *Google* because they never tell you how their formula works. In our *8-Second PR* book, you will find more details about *Amazon* book ad campaigns. The next steps in this section will also give you the highlights.

40. Hire an *Amazon* Ad Professional —To boost your book sales, hire an *Amazon* book marketing professional, especially if you are self-publishing. If you have a publisher, ask if they are doing *Amazon* ads for your book. In addition, ask about their budget. If your publisher has a small budget, be prepared to invest in *Amazon* ads as soon as their money runs out.

41. Write a Powerful Book Description —Using best practices and engaging sales copy, set up your *Amazon* book description page. You want to speak directly to your audience by highlighting the top 3-5 benefits for reading your book.

42. Create A+ Content for *Amazon* —Set up A+ Content on your *Amazon* book page. For the best results, hire a professional designer who can create eye-catching graphics to break up the text. These graphics are a great visual that can increase your sales.

43. Create Your Author Page on *Amazon* —Set up your *Author Central* page on *Amazon* with your headshot and short bio. This author page is very important for your book marketing and brand. It is a way for readers to connect with you as the author, and cross-markets all of your books on one page.

44. Start *Amazon* Ads during Pre-Sale Phase —Start your *Amazon* book ad campaign once your book is in a pre-sale mode. People have written detailed books on how to do *Amazon* ad campaigns. You can read these books, but I really recommend that you hire a professional instead, because it's complicated.

45. Select Unique *Amazon* Categories —Make sure you select the best *Amazon* book categories. Selecting the right categories is an essential step for making your book an *Amazon* Bestseller. Any book ranked 1-100 in a category is considered a bestseller.

To improve your rank, select book categories that have less competition. For example, for my *8-Second PR* book, I studied the categories for competitive books and decided to use *Media & Communications Industry* as a unique category.

As we wrap-up your Phase 1 Book Pre-Launch steps, keep in mind that our goal is to make your book marketing successful rather than to overwhelm you. In order for your book to be popular, it's especially important to do this first phase right.

Are you now ready to move to Phase 2, which has much fewer action items?

7.2 Phase 2: Implement Book Launch Month Promotions

Congratulations! You've done a lot of the hard work already to get your book ready for the world to read. Your book launch month is the most important time to boost your buzz, awareness and sales. Everyone likes things that are NEW —especially reporters.

So here is how you can maximize your book launch month promotions.

46. Send out Book Launch Day Press Release —Write and distribute a press release announcing your book on launch day. Along with a summary and the benefits of reading it, include your book cover, author headshot photo, book trailer video and relevant action photos. Then, share your news everywhere on social media!

47. Ask for Book Launch Help from Friends —To give your book a boost, make sure you get friends and family involved in the launch. They've watched you work tirelessly on your book, and you just need to ask for help. Email, text or call 50 close contacts to shamelessly ask them to purchase your book on a specific date (ex., Tuesday), and post a verified review on *Amazon*. If you do this step right, your book will become an *Amazon* bestseller overnight. All you need is a rank of 1-100 for any of your book categories. And don't forget to monitor if your book becomes a "Number 1 New Release" for one of your categories.

48. Record Book Bestseller Milestones —Watch your *Amazon* numbers closely during the first month of your book launch. If your book gets an *Amazon* bestseller rank and/or your page gets a Bestseller banner, take a screenshot immediately. *Amazon* changes these ranks often (It used to be hourly, and now it's updated daily). Don't miss the opportunity to capture your wins! Then share these milestones online with gratitude.

49. Launch Publicity Campaign for Niche Audiences —Expand your publicity campaign to attract more earned media coverage by targeting your niche subject areas. By now, you should have developed creative media hooks that emphasize how your book is unique and helping others.

50. Get Media Training —To maximize your interviews, make sure that you get media training from a professional before any major radio and/or TV interviews. You can go back to our Step 4: Media Training Booster chapter in this book for a refresher course.

51. Practice Your Top 3 Backstories for Interviews —Identify three key personal backstories connected to your WHY and HOW the book is helping others. Think about what stories will resonate the most. Then share these stories as part of a conversation during book interviews.

People really want to connect with human beings through the power of storytelling. Practice telling your stories in 2-3 sentences for a TV interview that usually lasts an average of 2-3 minutes. While you will have more time during a long-form podcast interview (20 minutes –2 hours), you must be able to get to the point faster for TV.

Media Example: *KGO ABC7 Mornings* San Francisco Live TV Interview

3 Author Backstories for *Election Day* Illustrated Book

Author Jonathan Bernstein shared his backstory during a Live TV interview on *KGO ABC7 Mornings* San Francisco. He created an illustrated board book called *Election Day* that was very relevant during the 2024 election year. It reminded us of a *Where's Waldo* book with everyday characters from both sides of the political aisle.

For this media pitch and interview, these three short stories were featured:

Story 1: From a personal perspective, the author explained that the 15 characters are based on his neighbors when he was growing up in San Francisco (which provided a local media hook). Each character had a backstory described in the book.

Story 2: The purpose of this book was to remind people to vote by showing what the characters are doing on *Election Day.* Most are NOT voting. While one couple voted early, others have everyday excuses for not voting, like getting their hair done.

Story 3: Jonathan created an illustrated book with no words to emphasize the power of visual storytelling. Personally, Jonathan speaks six languages, and believes visuals can be understood in any language.

These three short stories gave Jonathan's *Election Day* board book a lot more meaning and connection during this 7-minute interview.

52. Be Available for Interviews —Make yourself available for last-minute media interviews, especially during your book launch month. You should always try to be available whenever a reporter requests an interview (this tip is emphasized throughout this book because it's so important). While it's not always possible to accommodate a reporter's request, remember they are giving you earned media coverage—for FREE.

Media Example: National TV Interview
Re-arrange Your Vacation for Top Media Requests

For my dating book, *Smart Man Hunting: A Fast-Track Guide to Finding Mr. Right*, I was fortunate to have a national TV interview on the 4th of July, Live and in-studio at *FOX News Channel* in New York City.

My first thought was who will be watching on a national holiday? However, I did not hesitate to immediately say YES!

I was in NYC for a vacation, and quickly re-arranged my flight back to Los Angeles to make this date work. To my surprise, a lot of people were watching, and my book became an *Amazon* bestseller for the next week.

P.S., They invited me back twice for future national TV interviews, which is your ideal scenario.

53. Share Your Media Wins Everywhere —You also want to post any media interviews on your social media. This step is especially important to build buzz, credibility and sales. Make sure to tag the reporter and media outlet/show.

54. Accelerate Your Social Media with Video Shorts and Stories —Increase your social media content with daily posts that include more video shorts and stories to engage your audience. Use the Insights on *Facebook* or *Instagram* to identify the best time of day to post, and then share creative content during those timeframes.

55. Use 3 Consistent Book Hashtags —Use your top three hashtags on social media consistently for your book promotions. You might use your #BookTitle #AuthorName and #BookGenre. I can't stress the importance of this action item enough. You want to own your author and book brands online.

56. Increase Amazon Ad Spend —Ramp up your *Amazon* book ad campaign during your book launch month. Review your pre-sales campaign results, make adjustments, and raise your advertising budget. This action item may be done by you, your publisher and/ or your *Amazon* ad campaign manager.

57. Host a Book Launch Event —Organize a book launch event to call attention to this major milestone. Your event does not have to be expensive. In one case, an author client hosted an online discussion via *Zoom* on her book launch day. The same author invited people to a paid book launch celebration featuring a celebrity chef a few weeks later. Get creative, and have fun planning your event(s).

58. Set up Daily *Google Alerts* —To help you get notified the same-day via email every time you, your book and/or topic are in the news, set up daily *Google Alerts*.

Once your book has launched, focus on a minimum of a 6-month marketing campaign. The reality is that your book can be promoted for years with the right marketing strategy, topic and business plan. As a result, many of our author clients have hired us for 1-5 years. Remember, *PR is a marathon, not a sprint.*

7.3 Phase 3: Plan Post-Launch Campaigns for Long-Term Success

For your post-launch phase, let's take a closer look at how you can continually attract media coverage with book marketing campaigns.

59. Review PR Results to identify Best Long-Term Strategy — Schedule planning meetings with your marketing and PR teams to review the past six months. Identify what stories have worked best. Then brainstorm new ways to reach your ideal target audience.

60. Develop Your Post-Launch Publicity Calendar —While the most important time to promote your book is the first six months after launch, I've also seen clients successfully promote a book for over ten years. At this stage, you want to carefully map out a publicity calendar with monthly themes and topics connected to current headlines, trends and relevant days/months.

61. Focus Long-Term PR on Lead Generation —A long-term PR campaign is ideal for nonfiction books that are a "lead generator" for your business, product and/or owner/founder. If done right, you can drive multiple streams of income by establishing yourself as a thought leader in your industry.

Media Win Example: *The Business Journals*

The Law at Work Author Quoted in 44 Markets Nationwide

Goody PR was fortunate to be hired to promote a new book by Alan Crone, who is an Employment Law Attorney and CEO/Founder of *The Crone Law Firm* to promote his business and book, *The Law at Work: A Legal Playbook For Executives and Professionals.* The book had already launched, so we focused on developing a long-term book promotion plan to highlight Alan as a thought leader and expert in his field.

Fortunately, Alan got an interview with a national columnist who writes a regular column called *The Playbook* for *American City Business Journals*. As a result, Alan was quoted about a battle about overtime pay regulation changes. This national story was syndicated / re-published in 44 different cities across the United States.

In addition, Alan was quoted in another *American City Business Journals* columnist's story a few days later. This second story also got published in 44 markets in *The Business Journals*, providing coverage in a total of 88 pieces of content.

Not only was this author and CEO quoted in a top media outlet, the two stories reached his target market of business executives across the country.

62. Recharge the Business Plan behind Your Book —Once your book has been published for over a year, focus more energy on your big-picture business plan. Find new ways to generate income. Create a course, publish a journal version of your book, offer coaching services, get paid speaker gigs, create a new game, and more.

63. Consider Selling Branded Merchandise —Consider creating custom merchandise, too, that might include t-shirts, hats and sweatshirts.

64. Multi-Purpose Your Media Stories —After you have a media story published, make sure that you multi-purpose this content to extend the reach. For example, turn your feature print story into a video Reel. You can also turn a radio interview into a custom video using the audio and images. Post both of these videos on *YouTube* with a strong description with keyword tags. And definitely post your media stories on your website Press page.

65. Use Creative Storytelling on Social Media —To connect emotionally with fans long-term, use creative storytelling regularly. Post unique and relatable content about your life. Share trivia and/ or behind-the-scenes stories that may not be in your book.

65. Post a Video Storytelling Series with a Theme —To engage with your audience, post a video series that tells a story with tips connected to your book, brand and/or business. Post videos regularly to continually connect and attract more fans.

66. Start Your Own Podcast —Consider starting your own podcast to interview guests about topics related to your expertise. Your guests will share their interview, which can help you cross-market to new audiences. For example, in support of my *8-Second PR* book, I launched the *8-Second Branding: Getting to Your PR Wow!* Podcast.

While it can be overwhelming to start a podcast, consider hiring an expert to guide you through the process. For example, I highly recommend former Producer Jess Todtfeld and former TV Anchor Cheryl Tan, who are both podcast show strategists now.

67. Create a Speaker Reel —Once you've established yourself as a thought leader, you can put more energy into getting speaking engagements. Consider creating a Speaker Reel video that highlights any speaking gigs and top media credits such as TV, *Forbes*, or *Psychology Today*. Hosts want to see you in action, and a video can be a very powerful way to demonstrate how you can add value to their event.

68. Do a *TEDx Talk* to raise Thought Leader Brand —Consider doing a *TEDx Talk* to increase your thought leadership brand. This is a monumental step that is a dream for many authors. To get you there, find coaches, books and people who have done *TEDx Talks*. Start asking questions and attend *TEDx Talk* events in your area to learn more.

69. Submit for Multiple Book Awards —To give your book even more credibility, submit it for multiple book awards. There are many options for authors, including our Annual *Goody Business Book Awards* where authors can nominate in 1-50 categories online in eight book genres (Business, Health, Finance, Leadership, Marketing, Entrepreneurs, Self-Help, and Technology). Being recognized as an award-winning author also has many marketing benefits.

70. Review Your *Amazon* Results Regularly —You want to regularly monitor your *Amazon* rank, reviews, ad campaign and budget based on feedback and engagement. You should set a goal to get a minimum of 30 reviews in the first year, and 50 by the end of the second year. If you self-publish via KDP, you can also do book promotions where you give away your book for free to boost interest and reviews. This type of promotion is great for engaging readers with your content.

71. Update Your Amazon Book Description and A+ Content — Based on feedback from readers, your public relations team and honest friends, refresh your *Amazon* book description and A+ content regularly to see what connects most with readers.

72. Start a Movement to Make a Difference —To put more focus on your higher purpose, identify a new movement that you want to start. For example, find ways to give back by donating books or time to a specific group or cause. This step can attract award-winning publicity that recognizes your social impact.

73. Adopt a Charity for Your Book —Ideally, you should always adopt a charity for your book that is in alignment with your personal mission and values. Think about what matters most to you, and find relevant charities. Donate a portion of your book proceeds to your cause(s). For example, I donate a portion of my book royalties every year to autism and cancer research charities.

74. Start Writing Your Next Edition or New Book —If your book has been published for several years, brainstorm whether you want to write a new edition and/or publish a new book. Ask trusted sources for honest feedback. Brainstorm the new content that you want to share to decide which way to go. And as an extra benefit, your *Amazon* rank can actually get boosted if you have multiple books about similar topics.

75. Lastly, Celebrate Your Author Journey —Writing a book can be a career and business gamechanger for many authors. It's incredibly inspiring to help people through your words. So remind yourself how your book is changing lives. Celebrate your positive impact and media wins, every step of the way.

Congratulations! You now have the author marketing secrets that most writers do not.

Yes, it takes a lot of steps to write and publish a book, so please take your time to plan your marketing strategy and action items during these three publishing phases. Go back and review this chapter carefully as a refresher.

Remember, you want to be in the top 4 percent of authors who sell 1,000+ books.

You can be in the top authors category by applying what you've learned in this chapter. The only question is — are you truly ready to embrace your book marketing journey?

STEP 7: Your Book Marketing Booster Action Items Recap

As you wrap up this chapter, here are your 3 Book Marketing Booster Action Items to propel your author life forward.

7.1 Phase 1: Develop Pre-Launch Book Planning Steps

Your pre-launch book marketing planning phase is your most important step. It is 60 percent of the overall process, and is the foundation for your success as an author. Set up an Excel spreadsheet to track your author action items. Get help from writing coaches, invest in a marketing budget, hire a PR agency, hire book designers, create a digital marketing strategy, submit your book for reviews and start pitching your story to the media at least 3-6 months prior to launch.

7.2 Phase 2: Implement Book Launch Month Promotions

Your book launch month promotions should result in the most media interviews. To do this right, ask for help from friends and family, launch a publicity campaign to reach your niche audience, get media training, practice your 3 media stories, and accelerate your *Amazon* ad campaign. And consider hosting a book launch event to build buzz.

7.3 Phase 3: Plan Post-Launch Campaigns for Long-Term Success

After the first six months, do a review of your publicity campaign results. Develop your post-launch publicity calendar with monthly themes. Focus on developing a business plan behind your book as a lead generator for multiple streams of income. Define your higher purpose mission that may include starting a movement and adopting a charity.

TOP MEDIA BOOSTER:
Magnify, Measure Wins and Make Your Story Go Viral

I want to fly like an eagle.
To the sea. Fly like an eagle.
Let my spirit carry me.

–Fly Like an Eagle by Steve Miller Band

Are you ready to step up your PR game to get top media interviews that can reach millions? Using the skills that you've learned in this book, *Award-Winning Publicity*, you can get your brand story covered by major outlets — for free. It can happen very quickly or take years to get a Yes.

When national publicity happens, you want to be ready to magnify, measure wins, and make your story go viral using the 3 Top Media Boosters in this final chapter.

So look up, identify your top media wish list, and imagine flying like an eagle. An eagle signifies rising above your limitations, spiritual strength, and focus. It also represents courage, which is required for achieving any top goal in life.

Goody PR believes that you must be resilient, and manage long-term media relationships with care. You want to make sure all parties feel valued and appreciated, including the spokesperson, client, reporter and your team.

And if your pitch gets rejected, accept a "No" with grace and humility –and then figure out a new media hook. You always want to leave the door open so that you can send your contact new or revised pitches.

Let's take a closer look at these Top Media Boosters that extend your reach:

STEP 8: Top Media Boosters

8.1 How to Get National Publicity

8.2 How to Measure Your Big PR Wins

8.3 How to Make Your Story Go Viral

Get your highlighter out and take notes while reading this final chapter to learn more insights on how to get top media coverage on the *TODAY Show, CNN, NewsNation,* and more, along with print and radio outlets such as *TIME Magazine, Fast Company, People Magazine, NPR, ABC News Radio* and more.

8.1 How to Get National Publicity

If you're a publicist, marketing professional or thought leader seeking national publicity, your biggest challenge is to boost your story magic with a media hook that immediately connects with a reporter. Along with some good luck and great timing, you must find creative ways to stand out.

So what are the insider secrets for getting booked on top media?

3 Top Media Booster Secrets

1. **Turn a Local Hero into a National Story**

2. **Newsjack Headline News**

3. **Be Relentless about Follow-up**

For many reasons, I love both national and local coverage. When I published my first book, I remember my media coaches and publicists emphasizing, "Get on local TV first" and "Go home for your first TV interviews."

Please don't discount local TV interviews. With non-stop *Breaking News* on cable news, reporters often intensely focus on 2-3 stories around sensational news. If you are not talking about these top stories, it's much harder to get booked on national TV.

While everyone wants national publicity, many do not realize that the most trusted source of news today is actually LOCAL News.

Your goal should always be to build a library of earned media coverage that builds buzz, brand credibility, and ultimately drives business to whatever you are selling.

To show you how a local hero can turn into a national news story, let's look at a top media example.

Top Media Booster Secret 1:
Turn a Local Hero into a National Story

With the right timing, media hook and buzz, your local hero story can get you on *CNN*, in *People Magazine* or interviewed on *NPR*.

Case Study:
Local Hero Comeback Story on *CNN This Morning*

After securing many local TV interviews, radio and national print stories about *Warriors Heart's Command Center Executive Director Michael O'Dell's* story for a few years, his local story went national.

Based on input from the *Warriors Heart* marketing team, *Goody PR* pitched this local hero as the spokesperson for a timely "holidays and addiction tips story". O'Dell's inspiring comeback story resulted in 12 stories in the month of December 2025 - including *CNN This Morning* for many reasons.

The first reason was that the media hook was unique and inspiring. Michael had spent two Christmases in prison for substance abuse issues where he got sober. While on parole, Michael met the CEO of *Warriors Heart* at the gym, who offered him a job as an Admissions Advocate answering their 24-hour hotline. Fast-forward to today, Michael now runs the operations for their Texas and Virginia centers.

The second reason was that Michael had a lot of media experience, and was great in these interviews. As a result, I was able to share videos of Michael on TV to the producers so they could see that he was a powerful spokesperson.

When the stars all lined up, this local hero was put into the national spotlight to encourage others to reach out and get help if they are struggling with addiction, PTSD, and co-occurring mental health issues.

CNN This Morning

> Monday 6:20 AM EST LIVE Interview
> Total Airtime = 4.5 minutes total
> Total Reach = 1.1 million

Coverage Included: Live TV interview, CNN online story, *CNN* Reel (posted by *CNN This Morning* and the Host), *CNN* video post on Facebook

* * *

You always want to be looking for ways to turn a local news story into a national headline that is timely and relevant.

Now let's look at how you can get national publicity by attaching your story to a trending topic.

Top Media Booster Secret 2: Newsjack Headline News

Did you know that one of the fastest ways to get national media is through newsjacking? Media outlets tend to follow a news cycle where they repeatedly cover a breaking news story that is trending. While you always want reporters to do a feature story about your business, brand or book, they are more interested in finding expert guests who can comment on the top news of the day.

Bonus Content: Reporter Reminder about Top Stories

During a phone interview, former *KSAT ABC News* Reporter Jonathan Cotto emphasized, *Remember, Liz, if it bleeds, it leads in the news world.*

So to get booked on national news, top radio shows and in print publications faster, your best bet is to explain why you are a great spokesperson to comment on whatever headline news is trending.

Bonus Content:
Producer Feedback from National Cable News

When I pitched a timely story to a national cable news producer for *Random Acts of Kindness Week* about How Dr. Laura Gabayan scientifically identified Kindness in her study and *Common Wisdom* book as 1 of 8 skills that contribute to wisdom, below was the response that highlights the importance of newsjacking.

I'm not sure this is an easy fit for us right now, but I'm happy to run it by the team. We've been finding that segments with a strong hard-news peg tend to perform best for both the broadcast and digital audiences.

So while that feedback may sound harsh, at least it was honest. It also emphasizes why connecting to a hard news story will get your story covered much faster.

* * *

Goody PR has used Newsjacking to secure thousands of media stories, including major media interviews on every news network for our clients. You can do this, too, with the right story magic, unique media hook, tools, media relationships, and great timing.

Getting top media interviews is often about knowing how to position your story —at the perfect time —on the perfect day —with the perfect spokesperson.

To help you identify trends faster, set up *Google Alerts* about your subject area, watch and read the news every day and follow what key influencers are saying.

Let's take a closer look at a few Newsjacking examples.

Newsjacking Example 1: *BBC World News* — Pandemic Brewing

In February 2020, there were rumors and general confusion that a novel coronavirus had started in China – but no one really understood a global pandemic was on the horizon. Many global cities shutdown businesses and schools in March 2020, so this example shows how to get ahead of a story.

I had just returned from the *Sundance Film Festival* in Park City, Utah, in January, where my entourage relentlessly used hand sanitizer and wore masks on the plane. Few people were taking precautions at this time. Fortunately, no one in our entourage got sick. However, many friends who ran a gifting suite at this annual film celebration got really, really sick —and thought it was a just really bad flu.

Watching the headlines and *Google Alerts*, I saw this issue growing and pitched that Asset Protection Attorney, Bestselling Author and Corporate Direct CEO/Founder Garrett Sutton could discuss **How to Protect Your Assets if there is a Black Swan Event** that is unpredictable and out of your control.

As a result, the *BBC World News* show *Talking Business* with Host Aaron Helsehurst interviewed Garrett via *Zoom* from his office in Reno, Nevada.

The first major mobile industry conference was also canceled the day of this interview. As a result, the producers asked Garrett to comment on this breaking news.

So the timing of this interview was perfect with the perfect spokesperson.

* * *

Let's take a look at another Newsjacking example connected to a national Presidential debate.

Newsjacking Example 2: *FOX Business* —Turbo Tax Debate

To connect to headline news, Tax Expert, CEO of *WealthAbility* and Bestselling Author of *Tax-Free Wealth* Tom Wheelwright wanted to talk about the tax policies of political candidates during election years during our 5+ year PR contract.

I brainstormed with Tom to identify media opportunities. And as a result, Tom's analysis was published in many outlets, including *Entrepreneur, Accounting Today, GoBankingRates, MarketWatch, Inman News*. And then, he got a last-minute national TV interview that was a gamechanger.

I was consistently pitching Tom as a tax expert who could comment on the Presidential candidate policies to the same *FOX Business* producer for over a year. When then-candidate Michael Bloomberg commented that he could not go to *Turbo Tax* because his taxes are complex during a national debate, we finally got a call.

The producer called me the next morning at 7 AM PST with an interview request for Tom 3 hours later around at 10 AM PST / 1 PM EST.

I immediately called Tom Wheelwright, and he rallied to make this interview happen. He was asked to go to a remote studio in Scottsdale, Arizona, and was a Superstar Media Spokesperson.

Tom did not need a lot of preparation because he had done a lot of local TV interviews on this topic. I previously sent video examples of Tom to the producer, which included two previous national TV interviews on *FOX News*.

Overall, this *FOX Business* interview was a huge success. Tom LOVES taxes, spoke with confidence and conviction – and later got invited back as an expert guest.

FOX Business —Cavuto Coast to Coast

> LIVE TV 1 PM EST
> Total Airtime = 4 minutes 17 seconds total
> Total Reach = 128,836

Calculated Publicity Value = $50,115, based on a *Nielsen Media Report*

* * *

As another example of a timely story connected to headline news, here's a different story with a timely tribute to someone well-known

Newsjacking Example 3: *Boston 7 News and CW — Father's Day Tribute*

In sync with Father's Day, Rob Schwartz was interviewed by Boston's 7 News and CW, about his late father Morrie Schwartz (beloved subject of *Tuesdays with Morrie*). It was the perfect story at the perfect time with many heartwarming family photos.

Rob explained, "With the new book, *The Wisdom of Morrie,* posthumously published, this is my father's thoughts exactly… what he wanted to communicate with people…so I think this is the perfect way to honor him."

Morrie wrote *The Wisdom of Morrie* before he was diagnosed with ALS at age 75. The disease prevented him from getting it published.

Rob emphasized his father's message, **"The people who are important in your life, the love you shared with them, and the experiences that you shared with them - that's what's going to matter to you at the end."**

This story aired 11 times on Father's Day. **The Calculated Publicity Value was $47,425.00, according to a *Nielsen Media Report.***

The final PR Secret for getting top media is to be relentless with follow-up.

Top Media Booster Secret 3: Be Relentless about Follow-up

In many cases, the bigger the media, the longer it may take for your story to air or be published. While this delay will not happen with breaking news, a feature story can be put on hold indefinitely —or worse, never be published.

Your job as a public relations professional is to be relentless about follow-up, especially for print and podcast interviews that can take months to get published.

Media Example: *Fast Company*

Author Feature Story becomes Legacy Story

For a *Fast Company* feature story about *One Hit Wonder* Author Kevin R. Kehoe, I was relentless about making it happen. Here is the timeline, and an account of how one media hit turned into a legacy story.

May: I sent the first pitch email with two story options to a leadership topics reporter.

June: As a follow-up, I sent a new pitch idea a month later in June that Kevin wanted to talk about what to do if you get "thrown under the bus" by a business partner.

July: Finally, a phone interview was scheduled in July for Kevin with the reporter.

August: When this feature story was published at last in Fast Company in August, it was three months after the first pitch. Fortunately, the story also got picked up by *The Chicago Tribune's* Sunday issue.

September: And then, sadly, Kevin passed a month later after an 8-year battle with Stage 4 cancer (F-Cancer!). He was doing fine, but took a sudden turn.

As a sidebar, I was truly honored to work with such a brave client who wanted to keep doing PR until the end . . . to give back by sharing his message with the world.

To make a difference with the money Kevin received from the sale of his software company, he started the *Kehoe Family Foundation* to support several charities. His family chose the charities with him, including *Tunnel to Towers.*

This *Fast Company* story was highlighted in his obituary and life celebration. RIP Kevin R. Kehoe.

* * *

On a lighter note, many of our clients have praised me for my follow-up skills because I am relentless. Most of the time, my persistence results in a story getting published, but not always.

99% Publication Rate after Media Interviews

In 99 percent of the media interviews that I've secured over 20+ years, the stories have been published. When the 1 percent happens, it's not a great feeling, but you just have to keep moving forward. My intention here is to warn you that this does happen sometimes.

Maybe something came up for the reporter. Remember, you are dealing with a human being, who has life issues just like you. You may never know why a story wasn't published. And sometimes, you have to just let it go.

* * *

The key to your long-term publicity success is to be consistent, resilient, and relentless.

Never give up when you get a No, and remember it's ok to Fail Forward.

Yes, you will have bad PR days if you are a publicist or thought leader where you want to scream. And when this happens, make sure you take a time-out for self-care.

And yes, if you are a publicist, you will get high-maintenance clients who drive you crazy. Many will not appreciate your work, and that's doesn't feel good either.

My best advice is to stay focused on your higher level purpose —and keep going because you can change the world with positive press.

And create a support team of like-minded marketing professionals. I am truly grateful to have a coast-to-coast team of fellow publicists and PR agency founders. We talk every day to exchange story ideas, celebrate PR wins, and discuss challenges.

As an example of never giving up, *Warriors Heart* has praised my follow-up skills that were a success key for our long-term contract with them. During this 10-year PR marathon, I worked closely with their team to generate steady award-winning publicity results. To provide you with more insights, I will discuss the measurements in the next section.

8.2 How to Measure Your Big PR Wins

Once your interview is published, you next job is to measure your PR wins, a task which can involve reports for different metrics, using a variety tools. Many software and media companies offer different solutions because this step is so important for showing the value of the publicity.

Most of the best media measurement tools are paid versus free. So if you are a public relations agency, publicist and/or business owner, you should invest in these tools (see the RESOURCES section in this book for suggestions.) To be successful in PR, you must have a budget and tools to measure your bottom-line impacts.

If you are a spokesperson or author without a budget for marketing measurement tools, you can *Google* to try to find these numbers manually. While you will need to get creative with your searches for audience sizes, you can find their social media followers.

Let's take a closer look at different ways to measure publicity results, starting with business goals, and then specific measurements.

Measure Publicity Results based on Business Goals

You should always set goals at the beginning of a public relations program. While PR is just one part of an overall marketing engine, it can make a significant impact.

For our award-winning publicity campaign and public relations program for *APO/ Eclipse Glasses*, I asked about the company's overall goal as part of the strategy and planning. Please don't skip this step.

In this case, *APO's* top business goal was to sell 75 Million eclipse glasses for the 2024 Total Solar Eclipse. In comparison, *American Paper Optics* sold 47 million eclipse glasses for the 2017 Total Solar Eclipse across the United States. As a result, this 2024 goal was a 60 percent increase in sales.

PR Contributed to Mega Business Goals Success

As a result of 183 unique earned media stories, *APO's* CMO confirmed that *Goody PR's* public relations program "contributed to" the company meeting their Mega Business Goal to sell **75 Million eclipse glasses.**

Just imagine the impact of their positive publicity on the bottom line with those types of numbers and sales!

Measure Publicity Results based on Business Impacts

In a second example, *Warriors Heart* set up a specific 24-hour hotline phone number to use in all media stories to track the impact of their public relations efforts. *Goody PR* then literally begged reporters to include this hotline number and website link in every story, a challenge which is not easy.

Many media outlets have specific rules not to include this data because management wants to keep traffic on their website. Remember, you are seeking earned media versus paid media coverage, so you cannot require them to include your link or phone number. Overall, it's the outlet's story, so they get the final say on the content.

Usually, national media (*TODAY Show, CNN, TIME, NPR*) are much less likely to include an outside link. None of these top media outlets included a link to *Warriors Heart,* even though we asked several times. Because the top media often did not include this number or website, it was very hard to specifically track results by story.

However, there are other ways to measure potential impacts of media coverage.

In all cases, you should encourage your clients to track results in some way. It may be a simple survey question that asks, "Where did you hear about us?" If they mention a media story, then you have that feedback.

How to Measure Your Media Story Metrics

Another way that many publicists and PR agencies track results is by measuring story statistics. For example, below are five key metrics you can track using different tools:

5 Publicity Story Metrics

1. **Total Unique Stories — Overall and by Type**

2. **TV Airtime — Hours, minutes and seconds**

3. **Estimated Audience Reach — Get data from different sources**

4. **Calculated Publicity Value for TV — Earned Media coverage is worth 3 times the Value of a Paid Ad**

5. **Total Media Hits — Add Unique Stories and Online Syndications**

Let's take a closer look at how we measured three award-winning publicity campaigns and public relations programs using these metrics.

For a short 3-month book launch campaign, *Goody PR* had little time to prepare. The client hired us three weeks before the book launch, when a 3-6 month ramp up is recommended. In this case, I moved at warp speed to maximize results for the author.

For this rapid response, below is a high-level summary of the results measured.

PR Metrics Example 1: 3-Month Book Launch Program For Dr. Portia Preston, *Hustle, Flow, or Let It Go?*

Overall, *Goody PR* secured 40 stories for Author Dr. Portia Preston during this 3-month book launch campaign. As a result, the book had an average of 13 published/secured stories per month, when the goal was 2-3 stories/month.

The overall media totals were 333 percent higher than the goal.

To provide you with more background, here is a high-level summary:

26 = Unique Stories Published (plus 14 in process, so 40 Total)

- **1 = TV** (*FOX 11 Los Angeles*, 2nd TV interview request, but not available)

- **14 = Print** (*Psychology Today, Atlanta Tribune, Atlanta Daily World, Reviews*)

- **7 = Radio/Podcasts** (7 published,12 more in process)

- **3 = Press Releases** (one per month)

- **10 = Videos** (*Heal Podcast, Mind Over Matter* Video Short, *FOX 11 LA*)

- **887 = Syndications/ Republished** (including *MSN*, a 480k Reach!)

- **915 = Total Media Hits** (Stories + Syndications)

- **1.3 million = Total Estimated Reach/ Audience Size**

- (Note: It's almost impossible to find podcast data, so that is not included.)

- **$31,200 = Calculated Publicity Value (for TV interview only)**

PLUS —Events and Awards

- 2 Book Talk/Signing Events at Barnes and Noble Santa Monica and Barnes and Noble Huntington Beach

- Book Awards —Submitted *Hustle, Flow, or Let It Go?* (won 1 award so far)

- Secured National *Psychology Today* Column & edited first story

- Media Training provided

- Digital Press Kits (digital and hard copy) with Media One Sheet and Press Images

- On-site support at *UCLA* Orientation Event and Photo Coverage

* * *

If we look at a longer-term contract, here are the record-breaking publicity campaign results for *APO / Eclipse Glasses* Publicity Campaign that was the inspiration for this new book:

PR Metrics Example 2: 8.5 Month Award-Winning Program *APO* / Eclipse Glasses National Publicity Results

For our Award-Winning Publicity Campaign and Public Relations Program for *American Paper Optics*, below is a summary of the metrics presented in our executive summary that contributed to *Goody PR* receiving six PR industry awards.

Goody PR Executive Summary for National Publicity Campaign

Big Picture Results

- 183 unique Earned Media coverage over 8.5 Months that contributed to *APO* selling 75 million eclipse glasses.
- Positive, timely and relevant long-form content went viral.
- Quality coverage in a crowded, competitive environment.
- 54 TV interviews (16 national and 38 local) helped magnify this visual story.

National Media Coverage Highlights included:

TODAY Show, ABC World News Tonight, CBS Saturday Morning, NewsNation, Scripps News, FOX Weather (8 interviews), NPR, along with print coverage in *People, Forbes, WSJ, Memphis Business Journal* and more.

Overall Results

- **Total Audience / Potential Reach = 45+ million**
- **Total Calculated Publicity Value = $3.7 million (for TV only)**
- **Total TV Airtime = 8 hours +**
- **Total TV interviews = 54** (off-the-charts)

Total Unique Earned Media Stories = 183 (TV, Print, Radio/ Podcasts, Videos)

- Total Stories = 101
- Total Videos = 82
- Total Syndications/ Republished = 2,567
- Total Media Hits (total content created) = 2,759

Earned Media coverage by Type

- 54 TV interviews
- 39 Print Stories
- 8 Talk Radio/Podcasts
- 82 Videos
- Plus —9 Press Releases

PLUS —Digital Media Support

- Created Digital Press Kits with Photos and Videos for brand storytelling.

- Created pro-bono Digital Content (While social media marketing was not in our contract, we embraced the campaign, and could not resist posting videos as a value-add service.)

- Took hundreds of action photos at the *Albuquerque International Balloon Fiesta* during the 2023 Annular Eclipse Event that were later used in many media interviews.

- Created *YouTube Playlist* with *APO* TV interviews to enhance their SEO.

- Created 26 social media videos, and published as *YouTube Shorts* and *Instagram Reels*. These custom videos got 10,700+ views.

       ⚬ ● ⚬

As a third example, let's look at the 10-Year executive summary that I provided *Warriors Heart* as a final report for our long-term public relations contract.

To get these numbers, I went back to annual reports and files on two computers. It's really important to track results, and save the files. Every story is important, no matter how big the outlet. After some time, a media outlet may delete your story, so save copies of everything!

PR Metrics Example 3: Award-Winning Public Relations Program
Goody PR's 10-Year Executive Summary for *Warriors Heart*

As an example of how long-term publicity can add value to your small business, here are metrics for our 10-year award-winning public relations program. The heartfelt publicity contributed to *Warriors Heart's* bottom-line results and growth.

This consistent earned media boosted their brand's positive sentiment through unique and emotional storytelling.

Overall, these record-breaking results were a huge team effort with many inspiring stories featuring team members, milestones and timely themes.

As a high-level recap, *Goody PR* summarized their 10-Year PR Wins:

- **554 Unique Stories: Avg. 55+/yr, 1+/wk., 153% of Goal (Off-the-charts!)**
- **87 TV Interviews: $2.4 Million for TV Publicity Value***
- **13,000 Media Hits: Total Content = Avg. 1,300/yr (stories & pickups)**
- **48.6 Million Total Reach: Avg. 4.6 Million/yr (missing data on podcasts)**
- **Impact 1: Contributed to 4200+ Warriors at Warriors Heart**
- **Impact 2: Contributed to business expanding to second location**

*Publicity Value is for TV Only, and is based on Nielsen Media Reports.

To produce these results, I met with the *Warriors Heart* marketing team weekly to brainstorm media ideas. Based on feedback, I then researched and pitched national and local reporters based on different topics, provided their spokespeople with media training, gathered visuals for each story, and did a TON of follow-up with the client and reporters.

While these numbers are significant, the overall social impact of this Public Relations Program is immeasurable.

It was an honor to support *Warriors Heart's* mission to heal our military, veterans and first responders who are struggling with addiction, PTSD and co-occurring issues.

8.3 How to Make Your Story Go Viral

Now that you've gotten top media coverage, your ultimate publicity goal should be to make your story go viral. You want your online content (articles, videos and images) to gain so much popularity that people want to organically share your story.

You want your media coverage to magnify your story. Ultimately, you want reporters to start calling you for interviews and/or include you in a story because you're now recognized as the go-to expert on a topic. Sound good?

Let's take a closer look at some different tools and case study examples of stories that went viral.

How Press Releases Boost SEO and Online Pickups

While some publicists say press releases are a thing of the past, sending out press releases can help your story go viral by generating buzz, improving search visibility, and helping to secure media coverage.

If you have a newsworthy announcement, a press release can be a great way to amplify a new business, book, product or movie quickly. You can then take your press release and pitch it to the media for a potential feature story.

To send out a Press Release, you can choose from many different distribution options. Each platform has different costs and formats.

As best practices for format, make sure that your press release is about news versus just an opinion or statement. Use an action verb in the headline. Use the Associated Press (AP) style guidelines that include writing exclusively in the third person with titles and names versus pronouns. Avoid pronouns (I, she, he, they), unless in a direct quote.

While there are free press release distribution options, they will get no online pickups. Instead, you need to manually email reporters your press release and cross your fingers that they republish the content. I know publicists who still distribute via email using this manual approach for niche topics, but it's a much slower process.

If you send out a press release using a newswire, there are many options. The distribution costs vary greatly by platform. It's very efficient and professional. Your news story will then get automatically picked up online by hundreds of outlets.

If you pay for a newswire, you can also select several subject areas so that it is sent to a target list of reporters in your niche. For example, you may choose Business, Lifestyle, Health, Publishing, or Military as categories for your distribution.

Below are three press release distribution options that *Goody PR* has used successfully to boost client SEO quickly.

3 Press Release Distribution Options

1. *PR Newswire* —This is the top press release service and the most expensive. It will cost $800 –$1,300 for your first 400 words for a national release. You may pay more for additional words and/or to attach images. Our clients have paid up to $1,800 to send out one release on *PR Newswire*. I recommend using this service only for major news announcements such as a new company, book or film.

2. **Business Wire** —The service allows you to select a hyper-local, regional or national tier. The costs for a 400-word release range from $475 for local to $940 for a national release. As an example, *Goody PR* used *Business Wire* for a regional PR campaign for a client in Canada.

3. **EIN Presswire** —This option is cheaper, and has great media results. For a single release, the cost is $189 with a 700-word limit and one image. You can also pay $999 for one release with up to 2500 words and five images. In my experience, these press releases get an average of 200+ online pickups. They are connected to *Nexstar Media*, so you get pickups on local news websites from coast-to-coast.

Overall, all press release companies also offer discounted package rates. So if you are planning to send out several press releases, look for discount options.

Along with press releases, your news stories can contribute to your story going viral. You want to build so much buzz with positive press that reporters share your content.

Viral Story Media Examples

Let's look a closer look at some more examples of news stories that contributed to business, products and books going viral.

Viral Story Example 1: *CBS Health Watch*
National Feature Story Aired on 152 Local TV Outlets

In support of their grand opening, *Warriors Heart* had a feature TV interview that aired on *CBS Health Watch*. The story featured their new peer-to-peer addiction and PTSD treatment program that is exclusively for warriors.

For this national publicity story, the reporter and cameraperson visited *Warriors Heart's* ranch in Texas to pre-record the interview. They interviewed a clinician and an alumnus about their moving stories and insights.

While it was a short 2.5 minute story, this story went viral on *Veterans Day (November 11)* when it aired on 152 local *CBS News* TV stations across the U.S.

There were a lot of other stories in support of their launch, and this national media coverage heightened the awareness of this new program.

The Calculated Publicity Value for this one TV story was $633,573.

And the Total Reach or potential audience was 3.5 million people across the U.S., according to a *Nielsen Media* Report.

Let's look at a book example next that went viral as a result of several factors.

Viral Media Example 2: *40 Thieves on Saipan Campaign*
3 Reasons Why WWII Book went Viral

The World War II book, *40 Thieves on Saipan*, went viral across the U.S., Australia, and Saipan for three primary reasons:

1. **Untold Story** —WWII veterans did not discuss what happened when they came home from the war, so there was pent-up demand for this untold story. When author Joseph Tachovsky opened his father, Lt. Frank Tachovosky's, off-limits footlocker in the garage after he died, he found a treasure trove of discoveries. When the book came out 10 years later, every relative of every man in Joseph's father's platoon could not wait to read and share it.

2. **Entertaining Book** —Co-Author Cynthia Kraack worked closely with Joseph to turn his 600 pages of notes into a creative, nonfiction narrative that was a page-turner. The authors even studied movies, music and food of that time to create realism. The book also included priceless letters found in the footlocker.

3. **Coast-to-Coast Media Coverage** —As a strategy, I pitched stories in every city where platoon members and/or their families lived. Media loves to feature a hometown hero, and Joseph has historic photos of every man in the platoon. As a result, this 14-month campaign resulted in 15 TV stories, including on *Pioneer PBS, C-SPAN* and 13 local TV interviews from coast-to-coast over about thirteen months.

Print coverage included feature stories in *Leatherneck, Washington Examiner, The Oregonian, Minneapolis Star Tribune, Military Families Magazine, and Green Bay Gazette (3 stories)* and more.

For radio, Joseph was interviewed on the *National Defense Radio Show, John Carlson Show 570 KVI Show, American Veterans Show, WPR, podcasts and more.*

The 20-minute *Pioneer PBS* story that won an *Upper Midwest Regional Emmy® Award* really put the book on a national stage. As an added step, we arranged for the book to be exhibited in the *National WWII Museum*, where Joseph later gave a talk.

Overall, this historic book now has **1,100+ Amazon Reviews with a 4.7 overall rating**. It continues to be a bestseller, and Joseph regularly does speaking events.

❋ ❋ ❋

And as a finale, let's look at what made our award-winning publicity campaign for *American Paper Optics* / Eclipse Glasses go viral.

First, let's look at the coverage for Dr. Doug Duncan, who was one of their top eclipse expert spokespeople. As a result, his innovative *Solar Snap* product went viral.

Viral Media Story 3: *Solar Snap The Eclipse App and Kit* Astronomer, Spokesperson and Inventor Dr. Doug Duncan

Astronomer Dr. Doug Duncan was one of our top media spokespeople for the eclipse glasses public relations program and publicity campaign. As previously mentioned, Dr. Duncan invented *Solar Snap: The Eclipse App and Kit* that lets you take great smartphone photos of an eclipse. As you can imagine, his topic was very popular.

Overall, Dr. Duncan was a clear, concise, and compelling storyteller during interviews. Along with explaining eclipses with enthusiasm, he provided simple explanations and demonstrations of how *Solar Snap* worked.

Because he told this story in a fun way with great soundbites, Dr. Duncan's interviews got a huge amount of airtime (2 hours and 37 minutes total.) This airtime was primarily because his stories on *FOX Weather* and *Scripps News* were aired a total of 79 times.

For example, one of Doug's *FOX Weather* interviews about *Solar Snap* was just over 5 minutes. It aired 11 times, which was 55 minutes of total airtime for one interview!

Goody PR was fortunate to secure 33 unique stories for Dr. Duncan that resulted in 543 total Media Hits or online content for his *Solar Snap App and Kit.*

Overall, this media contributed to the product's story going viral.

And the *Solar Snap App* was the Number 1 downloadable app during the eclipse.

Media Coverage Summary for *Solar Snap Eclipse App* included:

- 4 National TV (*FOX Weather* 3x and *Scripps News*)
- 7 Local TV (*KSAT ABC San Antonio, Action News 5 Memphis 2x, KXAN NBC Austin, ABC Sacramento, KARK NBC Little Rock, FOX 2 Now St Louis*)
- National Print/ Digital (*Scripps News* with video republished on 61 websites, *USA Today, Red Carpet Report*)
- 16 Videos
- 3 Press Releases
- 510 Syndications/ Republished
- 543 Total Media Hits (total content published)
- Total TV Airtime = 157 minutes (2 hours 37 minutes)
- Total Reach = 1+ million

Building on this buzz, reporters automatically included *Solar Snap* in stories in *CNET, Forbes, Business Insider, The Wall Street Journal, Everyday Health, WBAL NBC Baltimore, KXXV ABC Texas, Daytona Beach News-Journal* and many more. I did not include these viral hits in our summary report because there were so many.

Overall, any publicist, brand or author dreams of getting a viral story with this ripple effect.

APO's interviews naturally built their credibility by featuring authentic eclipse experts, national publicity, and high-quality products.

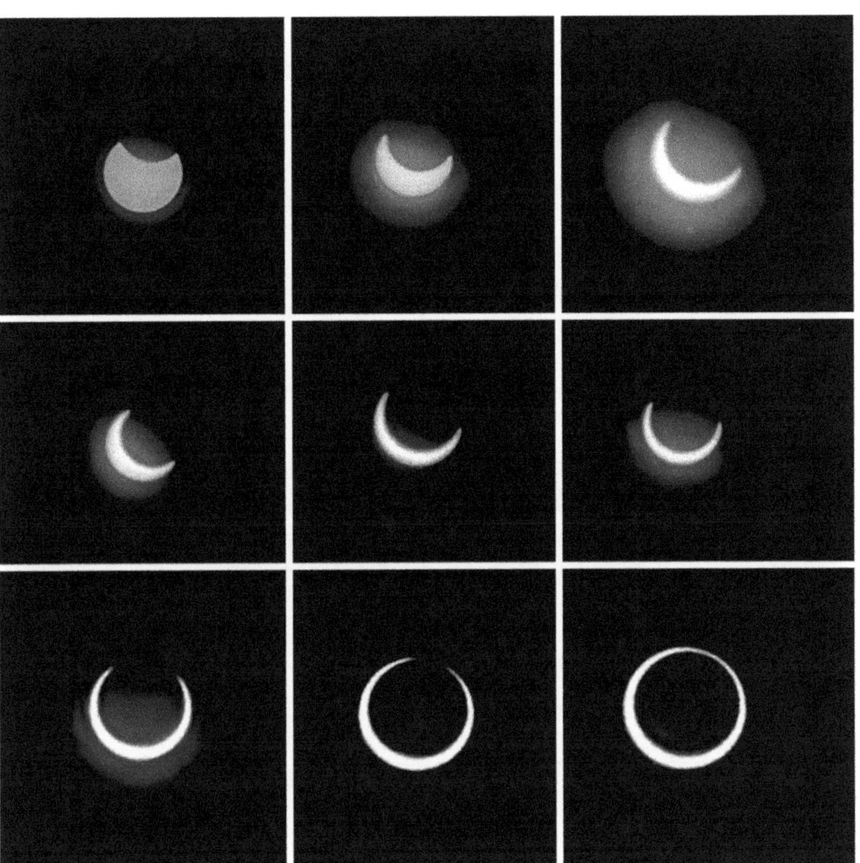

© Liz H Kelly photo taken with Solar Snap
The Eclipse App and Kit of the
2023 Annular "Ring of Fire" Eclipse at the
Albuquerque International Balloon Fiesta.

Media Example: *ABC World News Tonight* calls *APO* Eclipse Glasses Campaign Finale

For our Award-Winning Publicity and Public Relations Program for *American Paper Optics / Eclipse Glasses*, the story also went viral for many reasons. While our team had built a solid library of media stories, the campaign was boosted even more by the fact that the April 8, 2024, Total Solar Eclipse was trending.

Reporters were actively searching for credible sources and products to include in their coverage, and started quoting our experts based on previous stories.

APO quickly achieved their business goal to be recognized as the go-to company for the "best eclipse glasses" and "best photo app for eclipse."

During the first week of April, *American Paper Optics* had 23 TV interviews on air about their eclipse glasses (this is more TV coverage than most clients get in a year on TV.) Many of these interviews were pre-recorded, and outlets such as the *TODAY Show* and *CBS Saturday Morning* aired them during the final week.

Based on the buzz versus a pitch, *APO* CEO John Jerit was asked to be interviewed by *ABC World News Tonight with David Muir* for his *Made in America* segment.

During this segment, John and his *APO* team were featured while making and preparing to ship eclipse glasses. The b-roll video of their Memphis-area factory machines rolling was a perfect visual.

This national *ABC World News* story included three eclipse glasses manufacturers from across the U.S. *APO* was clearly the top company. At the time, they were making one million eclipse glasses a day to help millions of Americans view the upcoming "Super Bowl in the Sky."

Towards the end of their interview, John and his team proudly held up their eclipse glasses and said together, *"All of our glasses are Made in America."*

This interview was a monumental moment of pride and joy. It was the end of years of planning, and finding ways to survive the pandemic as a business.

Cheers to John Jerit (CEO), Paulo Aur (CFO/COO), Jason Lewin (CMO) and their entire *APO* team for working tirelessly to help millions safely view the 2024 Total Solar Eclipse.

While not every story goes viral, you should always measure and celebrate your media wins! Every national and local story can contribute to your overall success. Every story has a reporter behind it who took the time to tell your story —for free.

So please do a dance in the moonlight every time you get positive publicity.

You can now use these Top Media Booster tips to magnify and measure the impacts of your media wins, make your story go viral, and take your brand to the next level.

STEP 8:
Your Top Media Booster Action Items Recap Items Recap

As you wrap up this *Award-Winning Publicity* book, here are your 3 Top Media Booster Action Items.

8.1 How to Get Top Media Interviews

Identify 5-10 national Media Wish List outlets. And then pitch using the **3 Top Media Booster Secrets,** which include: 1: Turn a Local Hero into a National Story, 2: Newsjack Headline News, and 3: Be Relentless about Follow-up. And remember to use our mantra, "Be Patient, Persistent, and Never Desperate."

8.2 How to Measure Your Big PR Wins

Measure your PR Wins for a publicity campaign using our **5 Publicity Story Metrics** process. Quantify your Total Unique Stories, TV Airtime, Estimated Audience Reach, Calculated Publicity Value and Total Media Hits.

8.3 How to Make Your Story Go Viral

Use national media, press releases and impactful stories to make your brand go viral. Develop 3 creative media hooks with story magic to make your story fly like an eagle above intense competition. With the right Wow Story, you can naturally attract coverage.

In the Conclusion, you can review the Action Items Recap for all eight of the Award-Winning Publicity Media Boosters that you've learned in this book. Take time to give yourself cheers and celebrate every media win, no matter how small.

And if you are still reading, congratulations! You are now ready to jump into your award-winning publicity journey with new tools, tips and passion.

Fly like an eagle, and put a spotlight on your story.

CONCLUSION

Ooh child.
Things are gonna get easier.
Ooh child.
Things'll get brighter.

–*O-o-h Child* by The Five Stairsteps

As you wrap up this how-to get publicity guide, use this Award-Winning Publicity Success Roadmap and Action Items Recap to guide your brand onto a national stage. You've learned how to maximize results using 8 media boosters. It's now time to apply these new skills to your business, brand and/or book.

If you are a small business owner, brand, CEO, CMO, thought leader, marketer, and/or author, you can gain PR Value by applying these *Award-Winning Publicity* tips.

You now know 100% more about how to get award-winning publicity compared to 95% of your competition and fellow authors.

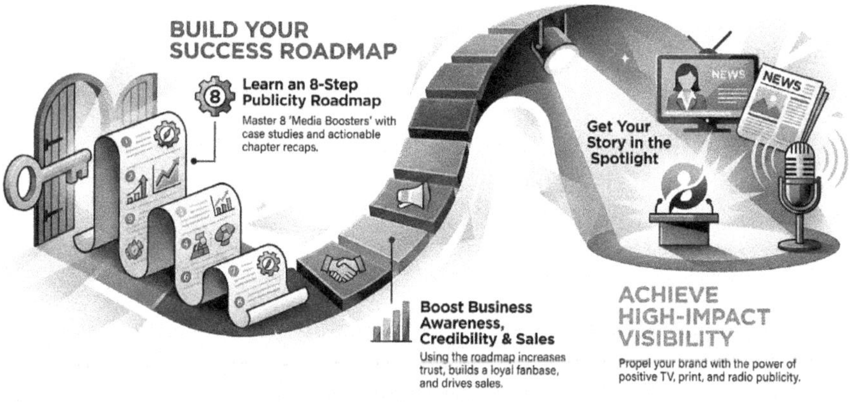

Use these insider secrets, and benefit from the three parts in this how-to do public relations guide:

3 *Award-Winning Publicity* Book Benefits

PART 1: Build PR Success Strategy - To set you up for success, use our Story Magic and Creative Campaign Boosters as a roadmap.

PART 2: Gain Positive Press Value - Get free publicity and increase your credibility and sales using our 3Ms: Media Outreach, Media Training and Media Relations Boosters.

PART 3: Magnify and Measure Wins - Make your story go viral with Digital Marketing, Book Marketing and Top Media Boosters. Measure your media and business wins.

PLUS: Bonus Content with reporter and expert insights.

Introduction: 3 Takeaways

1. What is Award-Winning Publicity?

2. What's in this *Award-Winning Publicity* book?

3. Why Resilience is a Must for PR Campaigns

As you map out your Award-Winning Publicity Success Roadmap, it can be overwhelming, so take your time. Go for a walk, brainstorm with your team and/or go on a vacation so you can find creative ideas to propel your story forward.

Identify at least one thing you can do each day to advance your story, increase your credibility and boost your business using the power of positive publicity.

P.S., And don't hesitate to contact https://*GoodyPR.com* if you decide you'd rather hire a professional to help you get national publicity versus doing it all yourself.

Let's now go through the 3 main points in each chapter, and your Action Items. Get out your highlighter again, define your goals/ objectives, and then create your master PR plan.

STEP 1: Story Magic Boosters

1.1 Define Your Diamond Ring Effect

1.2 Emotionally Connect with a Powerful Backstory

1.3 Research Trends and Competition to Define Your Uniqueness

STEP 1: Your Story Magic Booster Action Items Recap

As you wrap up this first chapter, look at your notes and determine your next steps for these 3 Story Magic Action Items. You can boost your brand and media results by applying these new skills.

1.4 Define Your Diamond Ring Effect

Go on walks, schedule a brainstorming call with your team, and then identify a unique Wow Story. Find powerful photos and/or b-roll video that can add to your story as visuals.

1.5 Emotionally Connect with a Powerful Backstory

Find an inspiring story that can entertain, educate and emotionally connect with your audience. Go back to your childhood or identify current events related to your story. Define what makes your story unique —with helpful tips and examples.

1.6 Research Trends and Competition to Define Your Uniqueness

Research relevant news stories and studies that connect to your story. Search for key statistics from reliable sources to support your pitch. And set up *Google Alerts* for your topic(s) to discover the latest headlines.

STEP 2: Creative Campaign Boosters

2.1 Define Your Campaign Goals, Objectives and Budget

2.2 Identify Strategies and Tactics

2.3 Develop Your PR Program Campaign Calendar

STEP 2: Your Creative Campaign Booster Action Items Recap

As you wrap up Step 2, use these 3 Creative Campaign Booster Action Items to boost your brand and media results.

2.1 Define Your Campaign Goals, Objectives and Budget

Work with your client to clearly define your campaign's big picture goals, theme, target market, and budget. Document these elements at the beginning of every campaign.

2.2 Identify Strategies and Tactics

Once you have your overall objectives, start working on a detailed strategy document with the Who, What and How for implementing your innovative creative campaign. And as a bonus step, include Influencer Marketing as a high impact tactic.

2.3 Develop Your PR Campaign Calendar

After you've defined the big picture publicity strategy and tactics, start researching your key calendar events. Put everything together on a shared Public Relations Program calendar so everyone is in sync.

STEP 3: Media Outreach Boosters

3.1 Research Top Media who will Love Your Story

3.2 Pitch Powerful Media Hooks with a Unique Story

3.3 Prepare Your Press Kits and Story Visuals

STEP 3: Your Media Outreach Booster Action Items Recap

As you wrap up this chapter, here are your 3 Media Outreach Booster Action Items to boost your brand and media results.

3.1 Research Top Media who will Love Your Story

Do some heavy-lifting research to find the best media who are most likely to fall in love with your story and topic. This research is an on-going process, but you have to start, so draft 3 Media Lists based on job title, outlet, niche, and geography.

3.2 Pitch Powerful Media Hooks with a Unique Story

To develop an Award-Winning Publicity Campaign, create 5-10 unique media hooks that you can pitch reporters. Use these media hooks to write a catchy email subject line that grabs their attention. Make sure your topic emotionally connects with story magic to get the reporters to say Yes.

3.3 Prepare Press Materials with 5 Key Elements

Prepare press materials with five key elements for each media hook, pitch and spokesperson. In your pitch email and press kits, send 3-5 Questions and Answers. Get your digital press kit set up on a *Google Drive* to share high resolution photos and videos safely. And make it really clear whom to credit for your visuals.

STEP 4: Media Training Boosters

4.1 Set Stage for Your Interview Success

4.2 Be a Great Visual with High-Quality Sound during Interviews

4.3 Use Storytelling and Soundbites to Connect Emotionally

STEP 4: Your Media Training Booster Action Items Recap

To help you use these skills, here are your 3 Media Training Booster Action Items. You can increase your media interview impact and results with great visuals, sound quality and storytelling.

4.1 Set Stage for Interview Success

Moving forward, you should prepare for every media interview by researching the outlet, reporter and potential questions in advance to ensure media success. Watch their TV show and/or listen to their podcast.

4.2 Be a Great Visual with High-Quality Sound during Interviews

To get ready for your TV and video interviews, think about what you are going to wear, your body language and how to vary your tone. Set up a quiet interview space with the best technology to enhance your message delivery.

4.3 Use Storytelling and Soundbites to Connect Emotionally

To increase your interview impact, use emphasis statements with three key points. Identify 1-3 short stories and soundbites that make you relatable and memorable.

STEP 5: Media Relations Boosters

5.1 Be Patient, Persistent and Never Desperate

5.2 Be Reliable, Responsive and Resourceful to Reporters

5.3 Share Sincere Praise and Appreciation

STEP 5: Your Media Relations Booster Action Items Recap

To help you apply these Step 5 skills, here are your 3 Media Relations Booster Action Items for your long-term success.

5.1 Be Patient, Persistent and Never Desperate

Create a list of your Hot, Warm and Cold Media Leads, and pitch them differently to build long-term media relations. While you always want to be patient with reporters, you must follow-up in a timely manner. It's a delicate balance, so view each relationship differently. If it makes sense, add your reporter follow-up action items to a *Google Calendar* with reminders.

5.2 Be Reliable, Responsive and Resourceful to Reporters

Set best practices for you and/or your client for how fast you plan to get back to a reporter who requests an interview. Remember, if you blink by waiting a few hours to reply, they may give your TV interview to someone else. Build your credibility by providing great guests, credible data and high-quality visuals to journalists.

5.3 Share Sincere Praise and Appreciation

Always write sincere and specific thank you emails and texts to reporters who cover your story, no matter how big the outlet. People appreciate being thanked for their hard work, and it can help you build invaluable media relationships.

STEP 6: Digital Marketing Boosters

6.1 Define Your Digital Marketing Strategy and Top 3 Platforms

6.2 Produce Video Storytelling Content that Educates and Entertains

6.3 Use AI to Maximize Digital Marketing and PR Efficiencies

STEP 6: Your Digital Marketing Booster Action Items Recap

To reach millions of potential customers faster, here are your 3 Digital Marketing Booster Action Items Recap to enhance your social media, video and AI.

6.1 Define Your Digital Marketing Strategy with Top 3 Platforms.

Document your big picture Digital Marketing Strategy that includes your goals and top 3 platforms. Define your ideal target audience, and focus your energies on where they consume their online content.

6.2 Produce Video Storytelling Content that Educates and Entertains.

Identify 3 video storytelling ideas as a series. Define three key topics for each video that can entertain and educate your audience. Schedule the filming and editing on your calendar for these videos.

6.3 Use AI to Maximize Digital Marketing and PR Efficiencies.

Identify three ways to improve your overall marketing workflows using AI, all while maintaining authentic human connections and integrity online.

STEP 7: Book Marketing Boosters

7.1 Phase 1:Develop Pre-Launch Book Marketing Strategy (Action Items 1-45)

7.2 Phase 2: Implement Book Launch Month Promotions (Action Items 46-58)

7.3 Phase 3: Plan Post-Launch Campaigns for Long-Term Success (Action Items 59-75)

STEP 7: Your Book Marketing Booster Action Items Recap

As you wrap up this chapter, here are your 3 Book Marketing Booster Action Items to propel your author life forward.

7.1 Phase 1: Develop Pre-Launch Book Planning Steps

Your pre-launch book marketing planning phase is your most important step. It is 60 percent of the overall process, and is the foundation for your success as an author. Set up an Excel spreadsheet to track your author action items. Get help from writing coaches, invest in a marketing budget, hire a PR agency, hire book designers, create a digital marketing strategy, submit your book for reviews and start pitching your story to the media at least 3-6 months prior to launch.

7.2 Phase 2: Implement Book Launch Month Promotions

Your book launch month promotions should result in the most media interviews. To do this right, ask for help from friends and family, launch a publicity campaign to reach your niche audience, get media training, practice your 3 media stories, and accelerate your *Amazon* ad campaign. And consider hosting a book launch event to build buzz.

7.3 Phase 3: Plan Post-Launch Campaigns for Long-Term Success

After the first six months, do a review of your publicity campaign results. Develop your post-launch publicity calendar with monthly themes. Focus on developing a business plan behind your book as a lead generator for multiple streams of income. Define your higher purpose mission that may include starting a movement and adopting a charity.

STEP 8: Top Media Boosters

8.1 How to Get National Publicity

8.2 How to Measure Your Big PR Wins

8.3 How to Make Your Story Go Viral

STEP 8: Your Top Media Booster Action Items Recap

As you wrap up this *Award-Winning Publicity* book, here are your 3 Top Media Booster Action Items.

8.1 How to Get Top Media Interviews

Identify 5-10 national Media Wish List outlets. And then pitch using the **3 Top Media Booster Secrets**, which include: 1: Turn a Local Hero into a National Story, 2: Newsjack Headline News, and 3: Be Relentless about Follow-up. And remember to use our mantra, "Be Patient, Persistent, and Never Desperate."

8.2 How to Measure Your Big PR Wins

Measure your PR Wins for a publicity campaign using our **5 Publicity Story Metrics** process. Quantify your Total Unique Stories, TV Airtime, Estimated Audience Reach, Calculated Publicity Value and Total Media Hits.

8.3 How to Make Your Story Go Viral

Use national media, press releases and impactful stories to make your brand go viral. Develop 3 creative media hooks with story magic to make your story fly like an eagle above intense competition. With the right Wow Story, you can naturally attract coverage.

And as you finish this book, remember, "PR is a Marathon, Not a Sprint." You want to find ways to track your "To Do" lists and take action to make your publicity goals happen, You also want to pace yourself, and take time to celebrate every media win!

As a PR, communications/marketing professional and/or thought leader, it's important to find balance. Push back on regularly working late nights, weekends or holidays. There are always exceptions for top media interviews or events, but try to protect your off-hours. If you are exhausted, it will be much harder to find the creative ideas you need to succeed doing public relations.

When asked how long you should plan for a publicity campaign for your business or brand, my short answer is that it should never-end.

You want your public relations program to be part of your long-term marketing strategy and budget for years versus months. Remember, earned media coverage is 3 times more valuable than any paid ad because someone else is vouching for you.

As a final step, consider nominating your work for awards to get third-party validation. You want to be known as an award-winning brand. The recognition can increase your credibility, trust and authority as a thought leader and/or brand. Submit for multiple awards for your business, thought leaders, books, publicity campaigns, and/or public relations program. And if you win, you know what to do —share it with the world —everywhere!

So go find your award-winning publicity eclipse moments, and email us your success stories and questions at info@goodypr. com.

And remember with the right creativity, strategy, media hooks, stories, tenacity and a little luck, you can become "Unstoppable" in your PR Marathon.

ACKNOWLEDGEMENTS

Thank you, Mom, for giving me your writing genes, and for editing this book. Your encouragement and quirky sense of humor helped me get to the finish line.

Thank you, Mom and Dad, for being my biggest cheerleaders along this journey.

BIG cheers to Jeannette for being the Best Sister in the World!

And many thanks to our family and friends (you know who you are!) for listening, being there, and encouraging me to never give up on our dreams —every day.

Thank you to our *Goody PR* Clients for your partnership, ideas, and gratitude. Your stories and positive impacts have inspired me to continue magnifying good.

Sending sincere appreciation and gratitude to every producer, guest booker, assignment editor, radio or TV host, columnist, blogger, book reviewer, podcast hosts, and influencers who interviewed me and/or our *Goody PR* clients.

Special thanks to the many reporters and experts who gave me personal insights for the Bonus Content in this book. Your insights are truly invaluable.

Thank you to my core team, including *Mary Rau Public Relations*, *Kathi Olson WPF*, Sudd Dongre, and many other publicists whom I've hired for client projects.

Special shout out to our three media coaches and mentors (Jess Todtfeld, Jamie Feldstein, and Roberta Gale), who got me started on the right track.

Thank you to PR and marketing pros who have been great sounding boards, advisors and team members for client projects over the past seventeen years, especially Grayce McCormick, Susan Bejeckian, Wendy Guarisco, Liz Dubelman, Ann Flower, Dr. Jess Neren, Tara DeWitt Coomans, Vanessa Diaz, Beth Okeon, and Richard Winfield Lewis.

Special thanks to Bill and Steve Harrison, who founded the *National Publicity Summit*, where I really learned how to pitch a powerful story to the media.

Thank you to Lee Ann Del Carpio for being our first ever client. Sending aloha cheers!

Special thanks to Lisa and Josh Lannon for being my PR partners on this journey as a VIP client for 15+ years for *Warriors Heart* and *Journey Healing Centers*.

Thank you, Tom Wheelwright and your *WealthAbility* team in Tempe, AZ. It was a true honor to constantly promote your educational products and services for 5+ years.

Lastly, special thanks to my book production team: Michele Weisbart (Book Cover Designer), Bader Howar (*Bader Howar Photography*), Shabbir Hussain (Interior Book Designer), Liz Dubelman (Book Publishing Coach), and my favorite former English Teacher a.k.a mom for proofreading.

RESOURCES

To provide you with marketing resources, below are suggested tools to amplify your publicity journey. Please visit our GoodyPR.com website for more tips.

This *Award-Winning Publicity* book has primarily focused on public relations tips for boosting your earned media coverage and magnifying your brand story. These tools and books can add value to your campaigns.

Media Outreach Resources

- *Cision* —A top national database of reporters used by many PR agencies (annual fee).
- *Muck Rack* —Another top media database with national contacts (annual fee).
- *PodSeeker, PodMatch, PodPitch, Matchmaker.fm, and Rephonic—podcast tools.*
- *Qwoted* —A Press Query service where reporters source experts for stories.

Email Marketing Resources

- *Constant Contact*
- *Mailchimp*
- *Sales Force*

Press Releases

- *Business Wire*
- *EIN Presswire*
- *Marketing Wire*
- *PR Newswire* —most expensive press release service
- *PR Web* —cheaper, and owned by PR Newswire

Digital Marketing Tips Reading

- *Mashable*
- *Social Media Examiner*
- *Social Media Club Los Angeles*

Social Media Management Resources

- *Hootsuite*
- *Sprout Social*
- *Hubspot*
- *Buffer*
- *Tailwind* —Instagram post scheduling

Photo and Video Apps

- *Adobe Photo Apps*
- *CapCut*
- *iMovie*
- *InShot*
- *iWatermark*
- *Canva*
- *Live Collage*
- *Pic Collage*

AI Tools

- *ChatGPT*
- *NotebookLM*
- *Rev.com Transcripts*

Marketing Books

- *100 Livestreaming & Digital Media Predictions, Volume 5 by Ross Brand*
- *How to Sell Books by the Truckload on Amazon by Penny C Sansevieri*

- *Media Secrets: A Media Training Crash Course by Jess Todtfeld*
- *Sobriety Marketing by Winston Bromley*
- *TAKEAWAYS: Ideas, Strategies and Encouragement for the Nonprofit Public Relations Professional by Marc C. Whitt*
- *The Social Shift: The Road Back to Community by Katie Brinkley*

Goody PR: Contact Us for Marketing, PR, and Social Media Marketing Services

If you do not have time to do everything in this how-to do publicity book and prefer to hire an award-winning PR agency, please contact us for a free introductory call: info@goodypr.com.

Check out our *Goody PR* website to learn more about our Services, and how we may be able to help you. See the Portfolio page for media examples of our latest work. https://goodypr.com

CLIENT TESTIMONIALS

Thank you, Goody PR and Liz H. Kelly for taking our 2023-2024 APO/Eclipse Glasses PR Campaign to the next level! Our record-breaking results for national and local media over 8.5 months, including 54 TV interviews, exceeded all expectations. This positive, long-form media coverage made our brand story timely and relevant . . . Working as a team was a wonderful experience, and I can't thank Goody PR enough for the amazing experience! We will be keeping Liz on speed dial for any future PR needs.

–Jason Lewin, CMO *American Paper Optics* / Eclipse Glasses

Working with Liz H. Kelly of Goody PR for more than 15 years—across both Journey Healing Centers and Warriors Heart—has been a meaningful and impactful professional relationship built on trust, shared values, and a deep commitment to mission. Long-term partnerships like this are rare, and Liz has been a consistent presence through multiple stages of growth, transition, and success. Liz's greatest strengths are her relentless follow-up, genuine passion for our work, and unwavering availability to our team—often 24/7 and even on holidays. I highly recommend her to any organization seeking a seasoned, mission-driven public relations professional who truly invests in the work and the people behind it.

–Lisa Lannon, Founder, *Warriors Heart Founder*

Kelly's PR efforts and innovative ideas have been an integral part of our marketing team's success for the past five years. After booking hundreds of media interviews, we had 900 Tax-Free Wealth books on backorder on Amazon. When our publisher asked, "What did you do?" we said, "Well, we hired a publicist." If you're looking for a great PR partner to promote your business, I highly recommend Liz Kelly.

–Tom Wheelwright, CPA, CEO of *WealthAbility* and Tax-Free Wealth Author

Thank you to Liz Kelly/Goody PR for bringing Hustle, Flow, or Let It Go? to the world. Liz earned my trust from the start by focusing on my authentic needs and understanding from Day 1 the value of my book's message and the impact it could have on the world. She wove my skills as a subject matter expert, entrepreneur, and speaker into a cohesive message that spoke clearly to outlets. Her media training equipped me to share that message knowledgeably in a relatable way. The biggest benefit of working with Liz is that everything we achieved together, from TV, print, radio, and podcast interviews, to book reviews, awards, and strategic press releases, will continue to serve me as I move forward. Liz is truly a treasure trove of experience, and I'm fortunate to have worked with her.

–Dr. Portia Preston, CEO/Founder *Empowered to Exhale* and Award-Winning Author *Hustle, Flow, or Let it Go?*

What I loved most about working with Liz Kelly on my book PR campaign was the way she was always brainstorming new promotion ideas with me and our team. She really cares about her client's success and personalizes pitches based on your expertise, relevant months/days and themes to make your story timely.

–Laura Gabayan, MD MS, Award-Winning Author, *Common Wisdom*

Liz Kelly's enthusiasm, creativity and teamwork approach all contributed to a PR campaign that went way beyond the goals set for my book launch. With over 40 media hits (interviews and syndicated stories), two speaking events and a Charitybuzz campaign for one of our book charities in 3 months, it was off the charts. If you want a PR pro who knows how to adapt and adjust to headline news to amplify your story, I highly recommend Goody PR and Liz Kelly.

–Danny Zuker, *MODERN FAMILY* Executive Producer, 5-time Emmy Winner and Author, *He Started It!: My Twitter War With Trump*

Goody PR has been a gamechanger for our WWII military history book 40 Thieves on Saipan about my father's US Marines Corps platoon in the Pacific. As a result of 2 PR campaigns, we were fortunate to have 13 local TV interviews, a 30-minute segment on PBS Postcards, a feature story in the Minneapolis Star-Tribune, and many radio interviews (National Defense Radio Show, American

Veterans Show). And our book reviews went through the roof on Amazon. We can't thank Liz H Kelly and her team enough!

–Joseph Tachovsky, Award-Winning and Bestselling Author, *40 Thieves on Saipan*

I'm grateful to Liz H Kelly and her Goody PR team for helping us promote our self-help memoir, Playing for Keeps - How a 21st century businesswoman beat the boys! —in the middle of the pandemic. As another woman in business, Liz continued to come up with creative ideas to pitch our career success story and money tips for retiring early. We were fortunate to get coverage in GoBankingRates, MSN, The Business Journals, MarketWatch, Yahoo! Finance, ABC Radio, VoiceAmerica Business Channel, The Secrets of Supermom Show, Raising Financial Freedom, a column in SWAAY and many more media. If you are an author, CEO or expert looking for someone to be passionate about promoting your story, I highly recommend Liz and Goody PR!

–Therese Allison, Successful Businesswoman, Award-Winning and Bestselling Author and Mentor, *Playing for Keeps – How a 21st century businesswoman beat the boys!*

If you're looking for a public relations agency that really cares about you and secures media interviews, we highly recommend Liz H Kelly and her Goody PR team. Kelly's innovative brand storytelling approach includes constantly connecting your topic to current events and headline news. As a result, I am grateful for an 8-minute timely TV interview about our Occupational Therapy tips and books that increased our reach.

–Sarah Appleman, Occupational Therapist, Consultant and Children's Book Author, *Paw Prints* series and *Playing With Your Food*

Liz helped Jukin Media with our initial launch party campaign, which included PR, social media and cause marketing for the Rob Dyrdek Foundation to reach our primarily 18-34 male demographic. This was a last minute campaign, and within 1 month, she helped us fine-tune our message, publish a press release, get key influencers to the launch party, and our social media fans increased on Facebook and Twitter by over 100 percent.

–Jon Skogmo, founder and CEO of *JUKIN MEDIA Inc.*, Los Angeles, CA (company sold to *Reader's Digest* parent, *Trusted Media Brands* in 2021)

@LizHKelly @GoodyAwards strategically helped us from early on thru launch to develop a global marketing campaign including press releases, social media and photography for @ComedyGivesBack 24 Hours of Comedy benefiting Malaria No More that contributed to our 100 million impressions in 2 weeks resulting in winning the IAWTV Best Live Event Award. We were thrilled to leverage the Comedy Gives Back platform to honor Budd Friedman with the Golden Goody Award.

–@AmberJLawson @ComedyGivesBack, Los Angeles, CA

Thank you Goody PR and Liz H Kelly for helping us take our brand story to the next level for our Personalogy Game! We appreciate the powerful storytelling process that you took us through to rethink our positioning in a more playful way that emotionally connects with the media, customers and retailers. As a result, we now have Walmart interested in putting our games in their stores for Christmas! We can't thank you enough!

–Michelle Burke, Creative Director and Co-Founder,
Personalogy Game

It was great to bring Liz back for a second social media training workshop at The Recording Academy (GRAMMYs) for local members and clients of MusiCares. There was a lot of positive attendee feedback for her 2.0 class which focused on increasing individual social media presence using Facebook, Twitter, YouTube, and Instagram. Her branding, popular music and Myspace examples were a big hit with the audience! There were approximately 40 participants, and Liz did a great job answering ALL of their questions. Thanks Liz!

–Brett Bryngelson, program specialist for *MUSICARES/GRAMMYS*

BOOK ENDORSEMENTS

Most people think publicity is about luck, connections, or hiring an expensive PR firm. It is not. In Award-Winning Publicity, Liz H. Kelly breaks down the exact strategies behind real media wins, from national TV to viral campaigns. This book will show you how to turn your story into a powerful engine for credibility, visibility, and growth. If you want more than attention, if you want impact, this is your roadmap.

– Jess Todtfeld, CSP, former TV Producer at *ABC, NBC, and FOX*, Media Trainer, Speaker, and Author, *Media Secrets*

Award-Winning Publicity breaks down how to elevate your story and your brand using smart, practical media strategies. Liz Kelly's eight Media Boosters, paired with real-world case studies, illustrate what works — and why — when it comes to building credibility, visibility, and results through positive publicity.

–P.K. Daniel, veteran journalist, whose work has appeared in publications nationwide, including the *Los Angeles Times*, *Washington Post* and *San Diego Union-Tribune*

Before working with Liz Kelly on our PR, I was famous only in Memphis. After Liz Kelly, I was world-famous. She knows her stuff. This Award-Winning Publicity book tells many of her secrets. If you want to know how to "get the word out," this book is a must read.

– Alan Crone, CEO/Founder, The Crone Law Firm and Author *The Law at Work*

Liz Kelly is the ultimate "Media Whisperer"! She knows exactly what it takes for a pitch to land. I love how she's organized each chapter with 3 key points — this approach mirrors exactly how journalists think, making it easier than ever to turn your message into a must-cover story. If you want to stop sending emails and start getting headlines, this is your manual.

–Wendy Guarisco, Founding Partner, CEO, Guarisco Group

There's a reason I refer my clients who need publicity only to Liz Kelly. Read Award-Winning Publicity and you'll learn the strategies that Liz consistently uses to take her clients to the top! This is the one read you need to increase your brand awareness, thought leader credibility, and trust —and attract loyal fans for your business, book or product!
– **Randy Peyser, CEO, Author One Stop, Inc.**

Publicity needs clear goals to translate purpose into visibility. In Award-Winning Publicity: 8 Media Boosters to Magnify Your Story, author Liz H. Kelly breaks the pursuit of media coverage into clear, actionable steps. Drawing on her award-winning expertise and client experience, Liz helps readers stop guessing, get focused, and align their media efforts with their intention, purpose, and goals. This is a smart, strategic guide for anyone ready to turn publicity into meaningful momentum.
–Debra Eckerling, The Book Proposal Expert and Author of *52 Secrets for Goal-Setting and Goal-Getting* and *Your Goal Guide*

Liz Kelly distills her years of experience leading successful PR and marketing campaigns into this immediately useful book. No matter the size of your operation, even if small, these practical tips will increase your success. Follow step-by-step as Liz explains how to create a successful marketing effort, giving examples such as her award-winning effort on behalf of American Paper Optics for the 2024 Total Solar Eclipse that crossed America. I was fortunate to be a spokesperson for our Solar Snap App and Kit, and work with Liz. You can make success happen using these publicity tips.
–Dr. Doug Duncan, Astronomer, *Hubble Space Telescope* team and *Solar Snap The Eclipse App and Kit* inventor

I have known Liz for close to 20 years; she is an expert at getting companies and stories highlighted in a busy and sometimes overwhelming media frenzy (just noise). It was remarkable to see how much media coverage she got for the Total Solar Eclipse. The insightful media examples and wisdom in this book will propel your brand. I highly recommend reading her new Award-Winning Publicity book.
–Carlos Cymerman, CEO/Founder, *Recruiting for Good*

Liz Kelly's Award-Winning Publicity is not just a book—it's a masterclass in how visibility truly works. Liz demystifies publicity and reveals what most entrepreneurs, authors, and experts never realize: publicity is not about chasing attention, it's about strategically positioning yourself so opportunities begin to seek you. What makes this book exceptional is Liz's rare ability to combine practical, actionable strategies with a deep understanding of messaging, positioning, and credibility. She shows you how to move from being one of many voices in the marketplace to becoming a recognized authority whose ideas carry weight.

As someone who works closely with authors, speakers, and thought leaders, I can say with certainty that this book provides the blueprint for turning expertise into influence—and influence into meaningful opportunities, media visibility, and business growth. If you are serious about elevating your brand, expanding your reach, and being seen as the expert you truly are, Award-Winning Publicity is essential reading.

**— Ruth Klein, TV Host, *The Book Club with Ruth Klein*,
7X Bestselling Author, Thought Leadership Strategist & Expert
Celebrity Branding and Media**

AUTHOR REQUEST

Please Write A Book Review.

If you found this *Award-Winning Publicity* book helpful, I would be beyond grateful if you post a book review on *Amazon,* in your blog and/or social media. A few sentences with your comments would mean the world to me!

Feedback is a "gift," and authors are especially appreciative of book reviews.

Your thoughts on what was most helpful can provide invaluable insights for how I can best help others do their own public relations!

If you post a review, please tag me @ LizHKelly so I can thank you. I will be happy to share and follow you, too.

LIZ H KELLY

ABOUT 8-SECOND BRANDING PODCAST

Listen to experts talk about the latest marketing, public relations and social media tips and trends on our *8-Second Branding* Podcast that is hosted by the *VoiceAmerica Business Channel*, and is available on all major podcast platforms (*Apple Podcasts, Spotify, Google Podcasts, Stitcher, iHeart Radio,* and more.)

We launched this marketing/public relations tips podcast to help brands like you better define your Wow Story in a clear, concise and compelling way.

Listen to our interviews with successful business leaders and authors who share their story-behind-the-story and marketing and promotion secrets.

Using the same superpowers of an unstoppable superhero, the *8-Second Branding Podcast* can help your brand be a force for good, build loyal fans and ultimately increase sales.

To listen, visit https://goodypr.com/8-second-branding

About Goody Business Book Awards

If you wrote a great book, and/ or know an author whose book is helping others, please nominate them for our Annual *Goody Business Book Awards*. Our mission is to *Uplift Author Voices* by calling attention to books making a difference —with words.

Any book published within five years is eligible.

Nominations are open October 1 –September 30, and it's an easy 5-minute process online.

When nominating your book, you will be asked: **How is your book helping others?**

You can nominate your book in 1-50 categories in these 8 subject areas: Business, Entrepreneur, Health, Leadership, Marketing/Sales, Money/Wealth, Self-Help and Technology.

Winners and Finalists are announced by November 15th —just in time for the holidays.

Authors, Agents, Publishers, Publicists, and Fans can nominate books here:

https://GoodyBusinessBookAwards.com

ABOUT THE AUTHOR

Liz H. Kelly is the Award-Winning *Goody PR agency* and *Goody Business Book Awards* CEO/ Founder, Bestselling Author of 3 books, including *Award-Winning Publicity* (2026) and *8-Second PR* (2022), Speaker, and Podcast Host whose primary mission is to magnify good through the power of positive publicity.

With 20+ years of PR and marketing experience, *Goody PR's* top media coverage for clients include the *TODAY Show, CNN, BBC World News, NPR,* and in *TIME, People,* and *Forbes.*

Kelly is a *Johns Hopkins University Carey School of Business* graduate, and a member of the *National Press Club.*

Follow @LizHKelly on *LinkedIn, Instagram* and *Goody PR's YouTube Channel,* hashtags #LizHKelly #AwardWinningPublicityBook #GoodyPRAgency, and/or visit https://GoodyPR.com or email us: info@goodypr.com.